ASKING
GOD *for the* GIFTS
HE WANTS
to GIVE YOU

ASKING

GOD *for the* GIFTS
HE WANTS
to GIVE YOU

Woodeene Koenig-Bricker

the WORD
among us®
press

Other Books by Woodeene Koenig-Bricker:

Praying with the Saints: Making Their Prayers Your Own
*365 Saints: Your Daily Guide to the Wisdom and Wonder of
Their Lives*
365 Mary: A Daily Guide to Mary's Wisdom and Comfort

Published by The Word Among Us Press
9639 Doctor Perry Road
Ijamsville, Maryland 21754
www.wordamongus.org
12 11 10 09 08 1 2 3 4 5
ISBN: 978-1-59325-144-4

Cover design by The DesignWorks Group

Library of Congress Cataloging-in-Publication Data
Koenig-Bricker, Woodeene.
    Asking God for the gifts he wants to give you / Woodeene Koenig-
Bricker.
        p. cm.
    ISBN 978-1-59325-144-4 (alk. paper)
    1. Prayer--Christianity. I. Title.
    BV220.K67 2008
    248.3'2--dc22
                                                        2008017687

For Matt: Just another part of the journey

Table of Contents

THE FIVE GRACES

Gifts God Wants to Give Us

St. Alphonus Liguori (1696–1787)

*Eternal Father, your Son has promised that you would grant
all the graces we ask of you in his name. Trusting in this promise,
and in the name of and through the merits of Jesus Christ, I ask
of you five special graces:*

*First, I ask pardon for all the offenses I have committed, for
which I am sorry with all my heart, because I have offended your
infinite goodness.*

*Second, I ask for your divine light, which will enable me to see
the vanity of all the things of this earth, and see also your infinite
greatness and goodness.*

*Third, I ask for a share in your love, so that I can detach
myself from all creatures, especially from myself, and love only
your holy will.*

*Fourth, grant me the grace to have confidence in the merits of
Jesus Christ and in the intercession of Mary.*

*Fifth, I ask for the grace of perseverance, knowing that when-
ever I call on you for assistance, you will answer my call and
come to my aid;*

*I fear only that I will neglect to turn to you in time of need,
and thus bring myself to ruin.*

*Grant me the grace to pray always, O Eternal Father, in the
name of Jesus.*

CHAPTER ONE

The Problem of Unanswered Prayer

Do you believe God answers all prayers?

You probably answered, "Yes, of course."

Does God answer all your prayers?

Now it gets a bit more complicated. If you're honest, you're probably thinking, "Well, I'm supposed to believe that God answers all prayers, but a lot of my prayers seem to go unanswered."

I agree. So why am I beginning a book on prayer by asking you to question if God really does answer all our prayers?

Because I know what answered prayer is truly like. I know what it's like to recognize that God is guiding my steps and arranging my life. I have experienced answers that have left me awestruck with the Father's might, power, and love. I want you to have that same experience, so I first want you to let go of your old expectations about how God answers prayer.

Is Silence an Answer?

We've all had times when we've prayed and prayed, and the only response we've gotten was silence. When that happened, you may have tried to convince yourself that God really had answered your prayer by answering no, but that explanation wasn't very satisfactory, was it? It didn't make you feel particularly loved or cherished by God as his beloved child, did it? In fact, it may have made you mad or left you disappointed or frustrated or discouraged. At the very least, it probably didn't make you want to keep on asking God for his blessings with confidence and conviction.

I don't blame you. I've had the same experience. I've prayed about something, received a stony silence as my answer, and then tried very hard to convince myself that the silence was God's way of saying no. Recently, however, I've come to realize that assuming that silence is God's answer isn't fair to God, and it doesn't do much for my faith, either. If I had been silent whenever my son asked me for something I couldn't give him, he wouldn't have been content. He would have kept asking and, rightfully, been upset if I had just pretended he wasn't there. To be a good parent, I had to answer him in a way he could understand; not just clam up and let him try to interpret my silence as a response.

Now, God is our parent, our good and loving parent. When we come to him in prayer, he doesn't ignore us and use silence as an answer. He always responds to us whenever we approach him in prayer.

So why doesn't it feel that way? Why does it seem that God so often gives us the silent treatment?

Why Doesn't God Answer My Prayers?

The reason lies, not with God, but with us. All too often we pray a prayer that God can't answer.

God can't answer a prayer? Heresy! God can do everything, right? Yes . . . and no. An old riddle asks, "Can God make a stone so large he can't lift it?" The question is impossible to answer. because the idea of God making such a stone is outside his very nature. Since there is no stone too large for God to lift, he can't create one. Such an action is beyond reality, and God is not only based in reality, he is reality itself.

While this can be a difficult concept to grasp, its implications are very real when it comes to our prayers. One of the reasons we don't get answers to our prayers is because what we ask of God is outside God's reality.

Let me give you an example. Once when I was very young (and very credulous), I wanted to wear a dress that I had long since outgrown. I lay down on my bed and prayed very hard that God would make me small enough to wear that dress one more time or, barring that request, that he would make the dress bigger. I really believed that when I got up and tried it on, it would fit. Of course it didn't, and I was quite put out with God. I had been taught that God can do everything and that God always answers prayers, so I could see no reason why he couldn't have expanded the dress (or shrunk me) for the occasion. But although God can do anything, and miracles do happen, an eight-year-old isn't going to fit into a garment made for a three-year-old. I imagine God shaking his head at that prayer, just as I did many years later when my son asked me, "What does blue taste like?" "Blue doesn't have a taste" wasn't any more satisfactory an answer to him than the silence and unchanging garment was to me. However, I couldn't answer my son's question because it was outside reality. My childish prayer couldn't be answered either because it, too, was outside reality as God has established it in this world.

Just a Tiny Miracle

Okay, you may be saying, but what about miracles? Don't you believe in miraculous answers to prayer?

Of course. I've even had a few experiences that I would consider pretty close to genuine miracles. But even when God performs a miracle, it's because he has suspended—not altered—one of his own laws. Let me give you a couple of examples. No matter how much you pray or how sincerely you believe in miracles, if you ask to be able to live in the court of Henry VIII or to be the first person to walk on the moon, it isn't going to happen. To grant those prayers would mean that God would have to alter every law of time and space—and that's outside the reality God has established.

On the other hand, let's say someone you love is dying of cancer. You pray and at the next doctor's visit, the tumor has completely disappeared. Is it a miracle? Yes, but this occurrence is still operating within the laws of nature that God has established. People do recover from illnesses. God may speed up or assist the process, but it's still part of God's reality to have immune systems destroy invading organisms. If that weren't the case, none of us would have survived our first encounter with the cold virus, and the human species would never have made it through the first night outside Eden. To be cured of illness by divine intervention is both a miracle and part of God's reality.

After all, it's God's universe, and we have to play by his rules. One of those rules is that because of the way he has set things up, some of our prayers just can't be answered. In effect, God has tied his own hands by the way he has constructed reality. He could have created a different universe, but he didn't. We just have to accept that.

"No-ing" the Difference

So what's the difference between a prayer God can't answer and getting no for an answer? At first they seem like the same thing, but they really aren't. When God says "No!" you know it. You experience a sense of closure and "rightness" about the outcome, even if you don't like it. Also, you have an unmistakable feeling of comfort despite the pain and frustration. The best example of a "no" answer we have comes from Jesus himself. When Jesus asked that the cup be removed in Gethsemane, the answer was an unmistakable no, but the Father sent an angel to strengthen the Son. Jesus didn't have to interpret silence for his answer. He knew the answer was no and, at the same time, he was comforted in his pain and sorrow (see Luke 22:41-44).

The same thing happens to us when God has to say no to us. We are comforted in the midst of our sorrow. Not long ago, my favorite cat fell ill, probably from being poisoned. I begged God to let the kitty live, but it was quickly apparent the answer to my prayer was going to be no. Even as I made the heartrending decision to end his suffering, I felt a sense of gratitude that I was with him at the end and that he didn't die alone in pain somewhere else. I also knew that God was grieving with me, not just refusing to answer my prayer.

On the other hand, when we pray for something that is outside God's reality—a prayer that he "can't" answer—we experience a disquieting sense of emptiness. We may feel upset, angry, frustrated, irritated, outraged, or any of a dozen other negative emotions. Even while we may try to convince ourselves that the answer was no, on some level, we know that our prayer hasn't been answered and it angers us.

If you have never experienced the comfort that comes with God's no, you may have never received no for an answer. Instead, you may have been praying prayers without the possibility of an answer. You have been asking God to tell you what blue tastes like.

God Really Does Answer All Prayers

Now that we've talked about the obstacles and misconceptions that get in the way of our prayers, let's talk about answered prayer.

Have you ever had the experience of praying and getting an answer that you absolutely, positively knew came directly from God? If you have, then you know the awesome realization that the Creator of the universe was listening directly to you. Once you've had that experience, you crave it again and again. You want to know that God is with you, always and in all things.

All too often, the experience is occasional, maybe even once in a lifetime. We begin to think that God doesn't really want to communicate with us on a regular basis. Yet we remember, and we continue to desire replicating that rare intimate exchange.

We ask ourselves how we can have this experience happen regularly in our prayers. What can we pray that guarantees an answer from God? How can we get God to respond? Is there such a thing as a prayer that will literally open the gates of heaven to allow God's blessings to pour forth on us?

Yes, such a prayer does exist. It's the Five Graces. Written by St. Alphonsus Liguori, an eighteenth-century lawyer who became disillusioned with corruption in the courts and left the bar to enter the priesthood, it's one of the little-known treasures of the Christian life. It's a prayer that God will always answer. Guaranteed.

This prayer consists of seven short petitions asking for five specific gifts that God cannot refuse to grant. That's right—this is a prayer that God absolutely will always answer! Sounds too good to be true, doesn't it? It isn't. The problem with our prayers is that all too often, we settle for less than God wants to give us. We pray with halfhearted hope, wanting God to answer and bless us, but afraid that he won't. Worse, we often fear that God doesn't really want to give us the good things we desire, but somehow likes seeing us disappointed. If that's the kind of God we think we pray to, it's little wonder we get so few answers.

It doesn't have to be that way. When you pray the Five Graces honestly and fervently, your life will change. It will transform your entire relationship with God. You will see God's hand at work in every aspect of your life. You will experience the confidence that comes from knowing God is hearing you, and you will feel his love pour over every moment of your life.

Although God will always answer this prayer, remember that prayer is a dialogue. You ask, God responds, but you have to listen carefully. As you pray the Five Graces, keep your heart and mind open. Watch for God's "still, small voice" (see 1 Kings 19:12, RSV) as it comes in ways you might not expect. Don't decide ahead of time how God will answer. Let his response be a surprise and a delight. When you do this, you will experience a radical new way of relating to God and recognizing his grace and power in your everyday life. Like a sheep, you will begin to hear and know your shepherd's voice.

The most transforming aspect of this prayer is that it will help you learn what it's like to pray in complete confidence that your Father in heaven is not only listening, but waiting to answer every one of your prayers, now and each day for the rest of your life. You will know what it's like to live in the midst of everyday miracles.

This prayer changed my life and my faith. It can change yours.

CHAPTER TWO

The Foundation of Faith

Eternal Father, your Son has promised that you would grant
all the graces we ask of you in his name. Trusting in this prom-
ise, and in the name of and through the merits of Jesus Christ, I
ask of you five special graces.

The Five Graces begins where all real prayer begins—with a
statement of faith: Eternal Father, your Son has promised that
you would grant all the graces we ask of you in his name.

This opening phrase might not strike you as being particularly profound or especially exciting, but it lays the foundation
that ensures that God will indeed answer our prayer.

How does it do that?

It establishes the essential relationship that we have with God
by affirming that he is our Father, not just during our earthly
life, but for all eternity.

If you've prayed the Our Father your entire life, as most of
us have, you may have become so used to calling God "Father"
that you no longer think about what that really means.

If God is truly our Father, then we are, by definition, his

children. And all children are dependent upon their parents. We think it abnormal and even sad when we occasionally hear about a child who is arrogant toward his or her parents or goes against their advice and guidance. Even if children become wealthy entertainers or members of royalty, no matter how much money they make or how famous they become, their mom and dad (or someone hired by their mom or dad) manage their money, make their business decisions, and guide their career until they become adults. When they try to take those matters into their own inexperienced hands, they almost always fail tragically.

So, in the very first two words of this prayer, we tell God that we know who we are . . . and who he is. We are his children . . . now and eternally. He is our Father . . . now and eternally. With those simple words, we admit that we aren't in control of our lives and, most importantly, we acknowledge that God is.

These first few words also remind us not just of our reliance on God, but of God's responsibility to us.

God's responsibility? What kind of obligations could the eternal Creator of the universe have toward us? More than we sometimes think.

If God had chosen to be our dictator or decided to assume the role of divine manufacturer in a heavenly assembly line, things would have been very different. We would have been slaves or worse, products. We could never hope to enter into a relationship with God because we could never approach him. Can a servant do anything more than follow orders? Can manufactured goods do anything except be packaged and sold?

Because God chose to be our parent, it is our right to make requests with the full expectation that they will be heard and answered. It's part and parcel of parenthood. For instance, if your child comes in and tells you he is starving, you will probably respond by getting him a sandwich and a glass of milk (unless it's ten minutes before dinner!). If a dog you've never seen before strolls in the back door, jumps up to the counter, and barks for something to eat, you'd toss him out the door. It isn't that you are an animal hater; it's just that a stray dog has no rights in your house.

We have rights because we are God's children. What an amazing thing to contemplate! God, the creator of all that is, was, and will be doesn't consider us objects, but his own beloved family. Being his children gives us the confidence to expect that he will care for us. It gives us the assurance that we can ask for our needs and be answered. By becoming our father, God has taken upon himself the responsibility of caring for us, his children. We are united, forever, because we are in this most intimate relationship with our God.

A Promise Is a Promise

The next words—*your Son has promised*—remind God in a sense, but more importantly remind us, of the promise Jesus made on our behalf: "Whatever you ask in my name, I will do" (John 14:13). We begin our prayer by calling to mind the fact that we have the promise of an answer—not just the hope, nor the wish, nor the desire for an answer, but the absolute promise.

A promise is a commitment that must not be broken. Think how angry and disappointed you become when someone breaks a promise they've made to you. Intuitively we know it's wrong on every level not to follow through with our word. God, who is incapable of doing anything wrong, will always keep his word. We can trust him implicitly.

Also contained in this phrase is the acknowledgment that it is Jesus himself, our Lord and brother, who made that promise on our behalf. Drawing on his unique relationship with the Father, Jesus, the Son, is able to make a pledge that God, the Father, must keep. While we are all God's children, Jesus is the Son of the Father in a unique way. When we say this phrase, we acknowledge the special unity between Jesus and the Father that we can share only through Jesus.

Next, this opening phrase provides the parameters of the entire promise—*all the graces we ask of you in his (Jesus') name.* One

way of defining graces is "every blessing we need." Graces aren't
all the material possessions or every object our greedy little hearts
and pocketbooks desire, but rather are all the blessings God has
waiting for us. They are what we need to become the authentic
persons God created us to be. The blessings we need are those
attributes, opportunities, and experiences that permit us to do
whatever it is that God wants us to do in this life. Now that isn't
to say that "all the graces" won't include material possessions. If
we are called to be a witness to the gospel in Hollywood, we will
need different clothes, transportation, and objects than if we are
called to minister to the poor in a third world country. The graces
we ask for are everything we need to live in such a way that when
we see God face to face, we are able to say humbly and truthfully,
"Lord, I have done what you asked of me."

One tiny codicil, however. In this prayer, we are promised that
God will give us those graces we need and request as long as
we ask in the name of Jesus. Expressing our faith in the Father
and in the name of Jesus involves more than just saying a few
"magic" words. We can't just mumble, "in Jesus' name, amen"
and expect it to suffice. Even the demons are said to recognize
the power of Jesus' name. Instead, we must acknowledge with
our hearts and minds that Jesus is indeed our high priest, our
intermediary, and that asking in his name really means that we
are asking him to take our request to the Father for us.

This opening statement of faith lays a foundation of trust that God is both all powerful and all loving. In order for our statement to have meaning, it has to say to God, and confirm in our hearts, the reality, "I believe you will give me all I need."

But do we really believe?

It's easy to be confident that God is going to give us all we need when things are going our way, when the future is bright and the horizon is crested with the gold of the good life. It's a lot harder to be confident when our life is in turmoil and we are facing uncertainty and pain. But that's exactly why it's essential to begin all prayer—in good times and in bad—with a statement of faith. It's our way of saying that we know that God is in charge of all aspects of our lives and that we truly believe that he will provide us with the blessings we need.

Of course, we have an idea of what those blessings should be, what they should look like, and even how they should arrive. But God has the final say, and more often than not, blessings come wrapped in odd packages.

Blessings in Disguise

Some blessings may seem to be anything but blessings, at first. Let me share a friend's story:

I've always believed in prayer and grew up praying in the name of Jesus. I truly believed in the power of his name, but then things happened that rocked the foundations of my belief.

My daughter had a son when she was just seventeen, dropped out of high school, lived with a drug dealer, and finally ended up having a daughter with a man several years younger than she is. Her boyfriend's whole family was involved in drug trafficking, but to her dad's and my sorrow, she married this guy, thinking they could get clean together. Of course, things went from bad to worse. He lost his menial-labor job and wound up in jail; and there she was, with two kids, no job, no skills, nothing.

I helped her as much as I could, but every time I heard about something else—his bad-mouthing a guard and being given more prison time, her failing to get yet another job, her son getting into trouble with the juvenile authorities—I fell into deeper and deeper despair. I couldn't sleep, and I began to have panic attacks. When I didn't think things could get any worse, her son was taken away from her and went to live with his birth father. Then she got in an automobile accident, and her husband was arrested for yet another crime spree.

At the very same time, I came down with a racking cough and fever that just wouldn't go away. Days turned into weeks, and I was unable to do more than move from my bed to my chair and back to my bed again. I went from doctor to doctor and was given the latest miracle drugs, but nothing helped. I had every test in the book, but all they could tell me was that it was "a virus."

My daughter would call me every day, begging for me to do something to help her and her family, but there wasn't anything more I could do. Some days I didn't even feel well enough to listen to her for more than a few minutes. On top of it all, I had been responsible for taking care of my elderly in-laws. My mother-in-law fell and injured herself. Because I was sick, I wasn't there to take her to the doctor, clean their house, or do their shopping. They were hurt because they felt I had let them down, and my husband was frustrated because his parents were so upset. He was angry at me for not getting well and then even more angry at himself for being angry.

I prayed and prayed that God would help, begging him in the name of Jesus, but it seemed like the more I prayed, the worse things got. "What am I supposed to do?" I would ask God. "How am I supposed to help them when I can't even get out of bed? Why don't you make me well?"

Then one day, after seeing yet another doctor and being told that I would get better "soon" and to "be patient," I realized that my being out of commission was allowing God room to work in my daughter's life. A situation I thought was going from bad to worse turned out to be the proverbial "blessing in disguise."

My grandson had been following in the footsteps of his stepdad, but once he got to his own dad's house, he started to turn his life around. He went to work at his dad's construction company and started taking classes toward a high school equivalency degree. When he called me after receiving his first paycheck, he exuded a self-confidence I had never heard in him before.

As for my daughter's accident, her car was totaled, but no one was seriously injured, and since the accident wasn't her fault, her insurance replaced the car. In fact, because the other driver was completely at fault, she got a settlement that allowed her to pay off some other debts, as well.

Finally, after her husband was in prison, my daughter told me about the things that had been going on in their life. I realized that she and her daughter were now in a much better situation. In prison, her husband could get treatment for his drug addiction, and their daughter was no longer in constant danger from the people who came in and out of their home.

The most amazing thing was that I began to realize that my own sickness wasn't God's punishment, but his blessing. I had railed against it, but I began to understand that being sick allowed me to back off, not just from my daughter's life, but also from a lot of other things as well. Because I was out of commission, my husband started taking his elderly parents shopping and to the doctor instead of leaving it all up to me. He began to see what I had been trying to tell him for months—that they needed to go to a retirement center. He had been able to deny the reality because I had been carrying all the burden. Now the burden had been lifted from me, and I hadn't even had to say or do anything! He saw that his anger had been misdirected at me; he knew deep inside that he wasn't doing what he should for his parents.

I realize that God had really given us what we needed, that my trust and confidence in our Lord was not in vain. My grandson had a new direction in life, my daughter got a fresh start and a car that runs, and I was even removed from having to take full responsibility for my in-laws. What I first thought was a terrible thing—my getting sick when my family seemed to need me the most—turned out to be the way God blessed all of us.

I would never ask God to make me sick, but now I see that being sick was the best way God could help all of us. I still suffer some side effects from all those months, but I no longer ask God to make me well. I trust that when the time is right, I will recover completely.

This happened a few years ago, and since then, my friend's health has been restored. She still struggles with repercussions from her family's decisions and lifestyles, but she says that she has finally learned to trust that nothing happens that God doesn't know about. And nothing can happen that he doesn't know is going to happen.

Often, it seems to me that God allows things to happen in our lives just so that we can learn to trust. In fact, trust is the next part of the opening statement of the Five Graces.

Ask . . . That You Might Receive

After declaring that we believe God will give us the graces we need, the Five Graces prayer goes on to be more specific: *Trusting in this promise, and in the name of and through the merits of Jesus Christ, I ask of you five special graces.*

It's not enough to remind God of his promise, nor is it enough to be intellectually aware of the promise. We have to put our money where our mouth is, so to speak. We have to expressly say that we believe this promise and make our request, because in saying the words, we make them real.

The spoken word has incredible power. The Gospel of John begins with the glorious sentence, "In the beginning was the Word, and the Word was with God, and the Word was God" (1:1). Creation came into being through the Word, and our faith comes to fruition through our words. We must assent to the promise God has made us, not just with our thoughts, but with all our actions, including moving our mouths and lips and saying the words aloud.

One of the biggest traps we fall into with prayer is that we keep it entirely mental. For prayer to be answered in the material world, we have to bring our prayer out of our minds and into our material existence. We must tell God that we believe his word, before we can allow him to act in our lives. We have to speak our needs aloud, not because God needs to hear the words, but because we do. Life coaches always tell their clients that saying goals aloud and writing them down are essential to accomplishment, because those actions access areas of the brain that make them more real, more concrete, and more believable. When we say our prayers out loud, we do the same thing. We use our physical being—our tongues to speak and our ears to hear—in a way that makes our prayers a reality to us. Speaking reaffirms our desires in a material way in the material world and helps us step out in faith. When we don't say the words aloud, it's all too easy to discount and discredit them even in our own minds, but once they are spoken, we can no longer take them back. Speaking aloud commits us in a way that mere thinking never can.

But we have to do more than just recite words. As powerful as words are, they must be rooted in faith. Unfortunately, our faith often wobbles, especially when we aren't used to having prayers answered. It's not going to work to put our trust in our own wavering faith and somehow expect an almost magical transformation from doubt to confidence. Instead we must put our faith *in the name of and through the merits of Jesus Christ.* When we have our misgivings—and if we are honest, all of us do from time to time—we put ourselves and our request in the hands of Jesus.

Jesus has done what we can never do—live and die in complete union with the Father. We can't do this on our own. We never can. But because Jesus has, we can hold fast to the merits he has gained for us. Because of Jesus we can approach the Father with confidence; because of Jesus we can believe with our heart, mind, and strength that our prayer will be answered.

Now that we have established our foundation of faith, we ask "five special graces." What are these five blessings that God cannot refuse to give us?

CHAPTER THREE

First Things First

First, I ask pardon for all the offenses I have committed, for which I am sorry with all my heart, because I have offended your infinite goodness.

What? The first grace is a confession of what we have done wrong? We already know we are sinners. What kind of an answer to prayer is admitting that we have messed up?

Think of this phrase as a sort of the "fine print" clause in the contract that must be fulfilled before we get into the blessings that God will give us. Before anything can happen, the matter of the pray-er's own spiritual state must be considered.

Psalm 66:18 says, "Had I cherished evil in my heart, / the Lord would not have heard." The prophet Isaiah is even more specific: "Lo, the hand of the LORD is not too short to save, / nor his ear too dull to hear. / Rather, it is your crimes / that separate you from your God, / It is your sins that make him hide his face / so that he will not hear you" (59:1-2). God makes it very clear that he cannot say yes to prayers that spring from an unrepentant heart. Because he can't give to us when we are in a state of sin, we must first acknowledge our transgressions. Then we can approach the Father with our requests. It's a little like a kid who has been playing in the dirt all morning. When it's lunchtime, she can't just come in, plop down at the counter with her filthy hands, and expect her mother to serve her a peanut butter and jelly sandwich. Her mother knows that if she were to let her daughter eat, her child might get sick from all the dirt and grime on her hands. So a good mother insists that her daughter wash up before having her meal, no matter how hungry her daughter is or how much her daughter whines and complains. It's the same with us. Before we get to come to God's table for the blessings he has laid out for us, we have to get rid of the dirt we have accumulated through our sins. So that's just what the first grace asks for—spiritual soap and water. We start by asking pardon for all the offenses we have committed.

Pardon Me

What does it mean to ask for pardon? The phrase "pardon me" has almost become synonymous with "excuse me." If we bump someone in line, we say, "pardon me" almost reflexively. At most we expect a polite nod. We certainly don't expect the person to make a big deal about it. It's just something we say, like "Have a nice day."

However, saying "pardon me" is a big deal, especially when we ask it of God. Asking for pardon isn't just social convention. It's legal language. Vestiges of its importance still crop up when a governor extends a pardon to someone on death row.

To ask someone for pardon means two things. First, it contains an unequivocal statement of guilt. By definition, an innocent person can't be pardoned. Only someone who has "done the crime" can request a pardon. So asking for pardon is simultaneously admitting guilt. Second, it implies that the person to whom you make the request has the power and the right to completely remove all punishment associated with a deed. It's important to note that forgiveness and pardon aren't exactly the same thing. Forgiveness is an act of the mind and will that frees the one doing the forgiving from hatred and anger. A convict on death row can be forgiven by his victims, but only the governor can extend a pardon.

When we come to God asking for pardon, we are admitting that we have sinned, and we are acknowledging that God has the power to erase those sins. We are also asking God to remove all trace of those sins from our lives and to restore us to our original purity. In computer terms, we are asking God to reformat our hard drives, not just erase the data we've stored there.

This first step is essential. Until we ask for pardon, not just forgiveness, God can't listen to the rest of our requests. So, we need to step up and say, "God, I'm asking you to pardon my sins. I know I'm guilty and I deserve punishment, but I'm humbly asking you to remove these sins from my life because you are the only one who can do it."

Shifting the Blame

When we ask God for pardon, we are guaranteed a "yes" answer. God will forget our sins. It's our legacy as God's children. End of story, right?

Well, sort of. There's a bit more fine print. It's true that God will erase our sins, but it isn't enough to saunter up and say, "Hey, Dad, hand over the pardon!" We have to have genuine repentance. If we don't, at best we're just mouthing words; at worst we are trying to shift the blame.

Let's be honest. Admitting that we've done something wrong isn't much fun. Most of us would prefer not to do it. And if we have to, we try to push a little of the responsibility onto someone else—sometimes even God! I know I've found myself waffling a little when it comes to confession: "It isn't really my fault, God. YOU made me this way. YOU knew that I was going to do this. So, I can't really be blamed!"

We try to do this all the time in our lives; we try to excuse our own failures by shifting the blame to someone else. After all, if we can prove that it's not our fault, then we can't be held responsible. Let me share a story with you from another friend that illustrates this all too well.

My adult daughter moved back to our town to escape an abusive ex-husband. Because she was destitute, I let her use my credit card to make some necessary purchases for her survival—shelter, food, clothing. She was very grateful, thanking me profusely when she brought the card back and giving me all the receipts. I put it in the safe deposit box because my husband and I use it only when we travel for business. When the bill came, I checked it against the purchases she had made. They all totaled up, so I paid the bill and never gave it another thought.

Several months passed. My daughter got back on her feet, got a job as a waitress, rented and furnished an apartment, and even bought a new-to-her car. When I asked her how she could afford all that on a waitress's salary, she laughed and said that she got the highest tips of anyone at the cafe. I knew that she was a very good waitress, so I didn't think any more about her lifestyle.

Then one day, I got a statement from the airline where I have my frequent-flyer miles. Much to my shock, it showed a huge surge in my miles. I mean *huge*—nearly forty thousand additional miles! When I called, I was assured that those miles had been credited to my account, but I couldn't figure out where they had come from. We hadn't been doing any traveling, and I hadn't made any purchases on the credit card that linked to miles.

A few days later, I visited my daughter at her new apartment, and there, on her kitchen table in plain view, was a billing statement addressed to *me* at *her* address. Since it was mine, I opened it and nearly fainted. It was for the credit card that I had lent her months before. The balance was almost fifty thousand dollars. I thought it must be a mistake, so I put it in my purse and didn't say anything. When I got home, I called the credit card company and learned that my daughter had switched the billing address from my house to hers and requested a duplicate card. She knew my mother's maiden name and my Social Security number, both of which are identifiers for being able to make changes on my card, so the credit card people never questioned her. Because she had changed the billing address, I was no longer getting the statements. And since

I wasn't making any charges and I had put the card in the safe deposit box, I wasn't expecting any statements.

Once she got the card, she was able to change the personal identification number so that she could withdraw cash as well as make charges. She had been buying everything she wanted, from her car to expensive clothes. The card had a very high credit limit because my husband and I used it primarily for our business, and she had maxed it out!

When I confronted her with the evidence, she was very sorry—not that she had used my credit card, but because she had gotten caught. "I'm sorry, Mom," she said, "but what did you want me to do? If Mike had been a better husband, I wouldn't have had to leave him. And if you and Dad hadn't been so critical of him I might not have married him in the first place."

I couldn't believe what she was saying! Then she went on to tell me that she couldn't really be held responsible for all the charges, because her new boyfriend's buddy had watched her punch in her PIN number and then had used her card to take one thousand dollars from the account.

I tried to be calm as I told her that she would have to pay it off, but she angrily interrupted and told me she shouldn't have to pay anything, because if I hadn't wanted her to use the card, I shouldn't have lent it to her in the first place. "It's your fault for giving it to me," she snapped.

When I pointed out that I had taken the card back and that I hadn't given her permission to change the billing address or the PIN and that I didn't know that she was still using it, she just shrugged and said, "If you want me to say I'm sorry, I will." Then she turned and said, "You know you can't do anything about this because I'm your daughter. You have to forgive me."

That kind of off-the-cuff demand for forgiveness doesn't have to be honored, because it doesn't carry any sense of remorse or any intention to change. God doesn't have to answer us when we come with a halfhearted story that we are sort of sorry for our sins, any more than my friend had to pardon her daughter's credit card theft—or pay off her bill, no questions asked.

The Conditional Clauses

How do we make sure that God will grant this first of the five graces—complete pardon of our sins? We have a couple of conditional clauses to fulfill.

I am sorry with all my heart.

We have to be sorry for what we have done. We can't just say we are sorry. We have to genuinely *be* sorry. That means we must acknowledge the full extent of our sin. We have to tell God exactly what we have done. without holding back. We have to have real remorse for our sinful thoughts, words, and deeds.

However, we don't have to be racked with great, gulping pangs of intense guilt. Genuine sorrow for sin isn't always accompanied by wailing and gnashing of teeth. More often than not, it's a steely-eyed look at our own sinfulness and an equally resolute recognition of our faults. If you don't feel remorse, don't try to conjure up some emotion just to try to convince yourself you're truly sorry. If you are really sorry, you know it—no matter what you are feeling. God knows the difference between crocodile tears that come from feeling sorry because we got caught and the genuine repentance that comes from recognizing our own sinfulness.

The second part of true sorrow is that we have to be willing to accept whatever consequences are our due, without whining, complaining, or blame shifting. Even if God pardons us for our offenses, we may still have to live through the consequences of our sins. Gerald Ford pardoned Richard Nixon for his role in the Watergate scandal, but Nixon will always be remembered as the only American president to have resigned from office. The pardon removed the punishment, but it didn't remove the stigma.

In the same way, God may pardon us, but we still have to live with the heart disease caused by our gluttony, the divorce created by our infidelity, the firing from a job due to our laziness. In order to gain the blessings God wants to give us, we have to be willing to say, "Yes, I deserve this. It is my fault, and I must accept the consequences of my actions."

Because I have offended your infinite goodness.

These seven words lie at the crux of our request for pardon. They are what ensures that God will grant us our request. We are pardoned, not because we deserve it, but rather because God, who is infinitely good, desires to give his children his love.

When we say this phrase, we are acknowledging our place before God. We are expressing our understanding that God has the right to judge us and therefore has the power to pardon us. We are humbling ourselves before our Lord and recognizing that God is all good for all time.

When we say this with our heart and being, God's power and presence surround us, and his love envelops us. God loves nothing more than to have his children come to him with a combination of confidence in his love and humility before his majesty. When we ask for pardon because we realize that we have hurt God, then God cannot help but grant us this grace.

Why We Need the First Grace

At this point, you might be saying to yourself, "Okay, so I'm sorry for my sins, I ask God for pardon, and he grants it. This isn't such a big deal, and it certainly isn't the kind of advice that I was hoping to get. What I want is a way to make sure that God will pay attention when I ask for help with my finances or healing when someone is seriously ill. I want to know how to change my life, not just get a rehash of something I've heard a thousand times before."

Let me share a secret with you that all the great saints have discovered. Asking for pardon is the first step in building a relationship with God. The only way that you will ever enter into an intimate relationship with God, a relationship where you experience God's abundance and blessing, is to first confess your sins. That's why the first grace is so important. It's what makes it possible for you to pray all other prayers and, most specifically, to ask that God's will be done in your life. Once you've asked for forgiveness, then you can begin to ask God to show you what direction he wants you to move in. Asking for forgiveness enables God to change your life. By simply and humbly confessing your failings, you put yourself in the place where God's YES resounds throughout creation.

Isn't that what you really want? To be in a place where everything works according to God's perfect plan?

Of course you do. That's what we all want, deep down: to be so in sync with God that what we want is the same thing that God wants. So begin now by asking pardon for having placed yourself outside of God's eternal perfect goodness. You don't have to don sackcloth and ashes or wail aloud on the side of the road as they did in ancient times. All you must do is sincerely and honestly admit that at times you have done the things you know you shouldn't have done and at other times you haven't done the things you know you should have. If you are in a state of serious discord with God, in what is called mortal sin, the sacrament of confession is literally a god-send. Even if you aren't in that state, going to confession can help give you the reassurance you may need that God has indeed granted your pardon.

However, when you sincerely ask and confidently believe, God will always extend this grace. Once you have confessed your shortcomings and failures, you are then ready to accept the gift of his pardon and prepared to receive the next gift God wants you to have.

Chapter Four

Light for the Journey

Second, I ask for your divine light, which will enable me to see the vanity of all the things of this earth, and see also your infinite greatness and goodness.

It's a little before dawn and I'm looking out my kitchen window. A cluster of orange marigolds surrounds a fountain cascading with water. Pots of purple-faced pansies nod on the porch. A basket of crimson geraniums swings in the early morning breeze. I know that the pots are aflush with brilliant color, but I can't see it.

At this time of morning, the world is suffused with gray. Marigolds, pansies, and geraniums are the same shade as the weathered deck, clay pots, and concrete fountain. Gradually, as the sun rises, the gray gives way, and the full spectrum of their colors is revealed. All I needed was more light in order to see what they were truly like.

What the sun does for nature, divine light does for us spiritually. Without divine light, we live in a shadow land where it's hard to tell what we should be doing or where we should be going; with it, we can see the truth for our lives and the direction for our future. God wants us see the truth so much that he has promised to give us the divine light we need. In fact, he wants us to have divine light so much that he cannot refuse to give it to us when we ask. It is the second of the five graces that awaits us, the second gift God longs to give us.

All we have to do is ask. Of course, we also have to be able to set aside our own preconceived notions of what the Light will reveal. Often it may not be what we are expecting. We think we know just how God will answer our prayers, and at times, we have decided exactly how we want him to answer them. When the answer comes in a way that we aren't expecting, we may not even recognize it as God's answer. It takes prayer—and an open heart—to see that God uses all things at his disposal, even what we would consider the most ordinary or even something we wouldn't choose for ourselves or our loved ones. One woman learned this truth when her daughter was diagnosed with colitis.

Miriam's Story

My mother had colitis, my brother has it, and both my daughters were diagnosed with the disease. The doctors are always surprised when I tell them that my mother died of it at age thirty-two because "no one dies from colitis." But she did. When my seventeen-year-old daughter Jennifer had a particularly bad attack, the doctors weren't all that worried, but I was concerned because of what had happened to my mom. I didn't want to lose her to the same disease—especially one that "no one dies from."

The doctors kept trying different medicines and nothing was working. Jennifer was getting sicker and sicker. Finally she was put in the hospital and the doctors admitted that she was very close to death. They told me that the only chance of saving her life was to remove part of her intestine.

I knew people with colostomies, and I knew how hard it was to have one. The thought that my beautiful, young daughter had to have either a horribly disfiguring surgery or die devastated me. I've always had what I thought was a strong faith, but I just lost it. I had been part of the healing ministry team at my parish. All my friends had been praying for Jennifer's healing, and now that wasn't going to happen. I felt like God had totally let me down. Why wouldn't God heal Jennifer, when so many of us had asked for it? Was that whole thing about "ask and you shall receive" just a lie?

My pastor came to the hospital to see Jennifer the night before the surgery. She was resting, so we went out into the hall. I leaned against the wall and began to sob, saying, "Jesus doesn't heal people anymore. That's just a story we make up to make people feel better. We've prayed and prayed for Jennifer, and nothing happened. He might have worked miracles two thousand years ago, but there aren't any miracles now."

Fr. Dom just looked at me. "If Jennifer has the surgery, will she be healed?" he asked. I paused. I hadn't thought about that. "Yes, but that's not what we wanted. That's not what we prayed for!" I said angrily. "We prayed for Jennifer to be healed, not to have surgery!"

"But," he asked again, "if she has the surgery, will she be healed?"

I drew a deep breath. "Yes," I said reluctantly. "That's what the doctors say."

"Then how can you say your prayers weren't answered?" he asked. "What do you really want? A miraculous intervention, or for Jennifer to be well?"

"His words stung. I had been asking for Jennifer's healing, but what I really wanted was a miracle. I had been so focused on the miracle, that I couldn't see that God was going to cure Jennifer in another way.

Jennifer had the surgery. She had a difficult time right after the surgery, but she is so healthy today that I can hardly believe it. The surgeon did a new procedure he had invented, and today Jennifer doesn't even have any external signs that something was wrong. She was healed—beautifully, miraculously healed—in body and soul.

It wasn't the kind of healing we had prayed for, but it was a total healing. I see now that God wanted to heal Jennifer, but when we were praying for a specific answer, it was hard to see that there was another way. God did answer our prayer—just not the way I expected him to.

That's how divine light works. Often it reveals a reality that can be very different from what we think we are seeing. Miriam and her family had assumed that surgical removal of Jennifer's intestine was a bad thing, when in fact, it was the method of healing God wanted to use to reveal his "infinite greatness and goodness." It took divine light—and a wise pastor—to help Miriam realize that God wanted to heal Jennifer, but that he would do so through the hands of a skilled surgeon instead of through miraculous intervention.

Mile by Mile

If divine light doesn't always reveal what we expect, what can we anticipate when we ask for it?

Once I was flying in a small plane at night. The pilots were using the freeway to navigate. Looking down at the ribbon of highway, I could see that the headlights of the cars revealed only a very small stretch ahead. From above, there didn't seem to be enough light on that highway to go anywhere, much less travel at high speeds. But down on the ground, the headlights revealed enough of the road for people to drive 65 miles per hour. They couldn't see for miles ahead, but they didn't need to. They could see what was immediately in from of them, and that was enough. All they had to do was focus on the patch of ground that was lit up, and go on from there.

God's divine light is like those headlights. It allows us to see just far enough in the distance to keep going right now. It doesn't give us the whole scene—just a pool of light that allows us to keep moving on our spiritual journey. When we ask for it, we will be given just what we need to understand and live in the present—no more and no less.

Vanity of Vanities

Divine light also shows us what the prayer of the Five Graces calls the "vanity" of things of the earth. For as long as I can remember, my mother had a painting by C. Allan Gilbert of a Victorian woman sitting at her dressing table, putting on her makeup. The woman is lithe and lovely, but when you draw back from the scene, you see that the dressing table, the mirror, the woman, and her reflection together create the optical illusion of a skull with hollow, vacant eyes. I have always been intrigued with the duality of the picture, which is appropriately titled "All Is Vanity."

Sometimes we think that vanity simply means inordinate concern with appearances, but vanity means a preoccupation with things that cannot last—like the beauty and youthfulness of the woman in the painting. In fact, vanity is even more than that. All the things of this earth are vanity. Nothing material will last into eternity.

As I write, I'm sitting in a cozy chair in my country kitchen, with a fire in the pellet stove warming the dreary Oregon spring day. An armful of lilacs perfumes the room, and the bell I put on my cat to alert birds of an impending pounce tells me that the mighty hunter has awakened from a nap and is strolling downstairs.

As pleasant as this domestic scene is, everything in it will someday be gone. Ten thousand years from now, the most that will be left may be a few artifacts for an archaeologist to discover and use to reconstruct life at the beginning of the twenty-first century. Maybe all that will be found will be the cat's bell—and with that, future archaeologists will create a whole scenario based on one little, insignificant item. The cult of the cat worshippers, perhaps?

Nothing that is so important to me today will remain. Vanity, everything around me, is vanity.

So why would we ask God to give us the ability to see the vanity of all things? Just so we can stock up on antidepressants?

Of course not. We ask to see the vanities of earthly things so that we can more readily see the value of heavenly ones. It's a little like comparing a rich imported French cheese with nonfat cheese substitute made from soy. If all you'd ever eaten was the nonfat soy cheese substitute, you might think that was as good as it gets. You might even rave about how wonderful one particular brand is over another. But once you taste the real thing, you know that what you had been eating, while not necessarily bad, wasn't really cheese.

It's like that with the things of the earth versus the things of heaven. When the world was created, God "saw that it was very good"—and it still is. It's just that the things of the earth are transitory—which is why they are vanities. We can still appreciate and enjoy the abundance of life, but once we understand that all the good things of the earth will end someday, then we can focus on the things that really matter—like seeing God's infinite greatness and goodness. That's why we ask to see what is vanity, before we become overly attached to it.

How Great Thou Art

Divine light allows us to become aware of the passing nature of all earthly objects. When we've gotten that far, we can also glimpse beyond earth into heaven, where we are able to perceive the infinite greatness of God.

My grandmother, who was Lutheran, often sang the hymn, "How Great Thou Art." Here are the first two stanzas:

O Lord my God! When I in awesome wonder
Consider all the worlds Thy hands have made.
I see the stars, I hear the rolling thunder,
Thy power throughout the universe displayed.

Then sings my soul, my Savior God, to Thee;
How great Thou art, how great Thou art!
Then sings my soul, My Savior God, to Thee:
How great Thou art, how great Thou art!

When we look around at the world, we cannot help but be awestruck. Even atheists admit that the world we live in is complex and beautiful beyond comprehension. With the aid of divine light, we can begin to see, not just the material objects that comprise our world, but the incredible greatness of the One who has created it all.

I sometimes wonder what the world would be like if we could truly see it the way God does. We know, for instance, that a whole range of color and sound exist that are beyond what humans can sense. Our senses are actually quite limited, so if what we can experience makes us gasp in wonder, we can't even imagine what God's reality must be like.

However, with the help of divine light we can become aware that God's reality is more than meets the human eye . . . and that God is a far greater God than we can ever imagine.

The Point of It All

Finally, with the help of divine light, we come to realize just how good God is. Through that awareness, we experience the awakening of a grateful heart. Then, as we become more grateful, we can enter into the abundant life that God has promised us.

How does this all work?

We say that God is good, but with the evil and sadness in the world, we often have our doubts. In one of the paradoxes of life, we can't see how good God is until we become grateful for his goodness. Once we become grateful, then we have more and more reasons to be grateful because we see more and more evidence of God's goodness.

So let's talk a bit about gratitude.

Expressing gratitude is necessary if we want to live the life God has designed for us. The universe runs on God-created laws. It doesn't matter if we like them, if we understand them, or even if we are aware of their existence. For instance, gravity doesn't care whether we have warm and fuzzy feelings toward it, or whether we can explain it in mathematical terms, or even whether we think about it at all. Apples fall from trees, the moon orbits the earth, and black holes suck up all light and matter without the slightest input from you or me. In short, gravity just goes about being gravity, with us or without us.

Likewise, one of God's spiritual laws is that gratitude allows God to give us all the gifts he desires us to have. In other words, gratitude releases his abundance in our lives.

It doesn't matter if we have consciously come to that conclusion, or if we have never even considered it, or if we have thought about it and ignored it. It's a reality, like the laws of thermodynamics or gravity. If we want to experience God's abundance in our lives, we first have to be thankful for all we have and all that happens to us.

Now sometimes people assume "abundance" means the mansion on the hill with the heliport and the Olympic-size swimming pool next to the tennis court. That's not what God's abundance is. God's abundance is everything that we need to live fully in his will and to become the person he created us to be—whatever that might be in terms of our health, finances, or relationships. No matter how much or how little we might have, we will always have enough when we trust God to take care of us.

Blessed Mother Teresa is a sterling example of God's abundance. This little nun in India had none of the things that the world counts as abundance. Yet with only two saris and a pair of sandals to her name, she saved thousands and thousands of lives, brought comfort to untold peoples all around the globe, met world leaders, won the Nobel Peace Prize, and inspired a generation who thought saints no longer walk among us. Her life was rich beyond measure, overflowing with God's abundance. Moreover, it was marked from beginning to end with complete thanksgiving for everything that happened to her. She was the living embodiment of St. Paul's admonition to rejoice always, pray without ceasing, and give thanks in all circumstances (see 1 Thessalonians 5:16-18).

Thanks for Nothing!

You may be saying, "Mother Teresa was a saint. It was easy for her to be grateful for everything. I'm not a saint, and I don't feel like giving thanks when everything in my life hits bottom."

That's where divine light comes in. We aren't told to give thanks *for* all things, but rather to give thanks *in* all things. Divine light helps us to see the difference. We aren't expected to be grateful because bad things are happening to us. That would be impossible. I don't know about you, but joy just isn't my natural reaction to bad news. I don't clap my hands for glee when the car breaks down or when my medical test results come back suspicious. I don't feel positive emotions. In fact, I feel downright unpositive ones.

However, with the help of divine light, we can begin to see that everything that happens to us in this life has purpose and that nothing happens to us that God has not permitted. We can begin to find things to be grateful for in the midst of the suffering. We don't have to be thankful for the suffering itself, but we can be thankful for God's presence in it. With divine light, we can find something to be grateful about even in those things that are painful or fearful.

Expressing gratitude in the midst of suffering was clearly shown to me when a friend went into the hospital for routine gallbladder surgery and came out with a diagnosis of cancer. When the type of cancer was finally determined, her first words were ones of thanks that it was a more curable kind than had been previously thought. She was grateful for a speedy diagnosis, for the pain medications, and once she was out of the hospital, for being able to sleep in her own bed. She wasn't grateful that she had cancer, but she chose to find blessings in the midst of fighting a dreadful disease.

If that weren't enough, a few days before she was to begin chemotherapy, her brother-in-law was found dead from a heart attack. He had been living alone, and when the body was finally discovered, the family wasn't allowed to see him. I'd have been downright unthankful at that point, but my friend saw only the good. "He died just the way he wanted to," she said. "In his own home." In fact, she helped her nieces create a memorial service that focused on the joy and happiness they had as a family, not the difficulties or the sorrow of dealing with what was a horrendous situation.

Her experiences were eye opening for me. I began to see that it really is possible to express gratitude in the midst of suffering, while not being at all thankful for the suffering itself.

That really is the point of this part of the Five Graces. We ask for divine light in order to see the vanity of all the things of this earth. We ask for divine light so that when we are wrapped up in what's happening in our lives, we can step aside and see that in the midst of what may appear to be the worst possible event, blessings abound. We seek divine light so that we have the strength to focus on the good that comes from a God who is all good. Finally, we ask for divine light so that we might experience freedom from worry, total peace of mind, and complete confidence in the future.

In fact, that's exactly what the next grace is all about.

CHAPTER FIVE

The Key to Answered Prayer

Third, I ask for a share in your love, so that I can detach myself from all creatures, especially from myself, and love only your holy will.

Who wouldn't want freedom from worry, total peace of mind, and complete confidence in the future? Who thinks that's actually possible?

It is possible, but like so many other aspects of our spiritual journey, perhaps not exactly the way we imagine it will be.

As long as we live here on earth, we will experience suffering. That's a given. However, suffering doesn't mean that we have to be worried, depressed, or afraid. Those emotions aren't conducive to spiritual growth. On the contrary, they can actually hinder our development.

Sometimes we suffer because we become overly attached to things, and their loss may even take us quite by surprise. I had a favorite mug that I used for my morning coffee for many years. When it cracked in the dishwasher, I was extremely unhappy. Coffee didn't taste the same for several days, and every time I poured a cup, I felt a wave of anger and sadness. I was overly attached to that blue and white mug.

Sometimes we are overly attached to our dreams. We've all seen pictures of movie stars who undergo so much plastic surgery as to be virtually unrecognizable, in a vain attempt to remain youthful. They are so attached to the image of youth and beauty, they cannot accept the changes in their own bodies.

And sometimes we are overly attached to people. Of course we are attached, and should be, to the people we love, but even that love can become excessive. I knew a man who was so attached to his wife that when she died, he spent all day sitting at her graveside, until about a year later, he finally died, leaving his children and grandchildren heartbroken.

Learning to Let Go

Learning to detach from objects takes discipline, but it is possible to do so without too much—if any—help from God. I've known atheists who have the attitude, "It's only a material possession," which serves them well when something is lost, broken, or stolen. Their lack of belief in a higher power has no effect on their ability to let go of material objects.

What can be more difficult, sometimes almost impossible to let go of without God's help, are living beings. When my beloved cat fell ill and then died less than seventeen hours later, I was racked with grief—and he was only a cat. Letting go of people is even more difficult, even when death isn't involved. For almost a year, I worked out with a trainer at my gym. When he was transferred, I was surprised at just how attached to him and his encouragement I had become. Going to the gym became a very sad event for several weeks.

Of course, God wants us to love other people; it's only natural that we grieve and suffer when we lose them. However, of all the things we need to be detached from, the primal one is our self-indulgence. We cling to our image of self, to our desires, to our wishes. That's why in this third request, we ask that we detach from all creatures, especially ourselves.

Detachment isn't easy. Ever try to hold water in your fist? The tighter you squeeze, the less you can hold. It's only when you let go and open up your palm that you can actually hold any liquid. By releasing your stranglehold on the water, you don't stop caring about having the water; you don't stop wanting to scoop up the water; you don't give up on carrying the water. In order to have the water, you must do what is intuitively contrary to expectations. Normally, when you want to hold onto something, you grip it tighter, but that won't work with water. It's only when you open your hand that the liquid will stay in it.

Detachment in the spiritual sense is similar. It entails relinquishing our grip on our specific desires while, at the same time, continuing to care about them, sometimes very intently. It's one of the least intuitive acts of our nature, but learning how to detach lies at the heart of our relationship with God. Without detachment, we block God's work in our lives. God cannot give us the gifts he has for us. With detachment, we open a space in our being that allows God to work miracles in our lives.

It might sound like I've mastered this skill. Far from it. Learning how to detach has been excruciatingly difficult for me. My close friends tell me that God has to pry my fingers from the doorjambs of my life with a crowbar before I'm willing to let go of people, situations, and events. Unfortunately, there's a certain amount of truth to their claims.

I am learning how to detach, however. I got a crash course when, after many years doing a job that I loved and found fulfilling, I felt an unrelenting inner call to leave that secure path and find a new road. I was terrified. How would I pay the bills? What would I do? How would I know if I was doing the right thing?

With a deep breath and a leap of faith, I quit my position without knowing what my next job was going to be. Then, in what seemed like a miracle, the ideal position opened up. I needed the income; the job was one that I knew I could do; it was with people I liked. I wanted the job for a number of reasons, not least of which was that it would touch a lot of lives and have the potential to bring great honor and glory to God. So I prayed, not that God would give me the job, but that the best person for the job would be chosen. Even I was surprised that I could pray that prayer with complete assurance, but with the help of the third grace, I succeeded.

I had great hope that I would be the best person, but my desire that the right candidate be chosen took precedence over my desire to get the position. I had confidence that no matter what happened, the outcome was in God's hands, and the right choice would be made. If I were selected, I would be delighted. If I weren't selected, I would be genuinely glad that the right person had been.

Now this might sound like pious prattle, but it wasn't. I turned the outcome of the situation completely over to God (something I don't do nearly often enough). I cared—a lot—about the job and my finances, but at the same time I was completely at peace about the outcome. I prayed, trusting that God would guide the decision. I was completely willing to accept the outcome, either way.

To Care or Not to Care

Oh yeah, you may be saying. That's a bunch of hooey. How can you care about something and not care about it at the same time? That's just religious babble. Either you care or you don't.

As unbelievable as it may sound, one really can care passionately about something and, at the same time, be confident that all outcomes will be equally satisfactory. I'd like to be able to tell you that I do this all the time, but I don't. Most of the time, I make a fist and squeeze the water in my life as tightly as possible, and then I am dismayed when I discover that my hand is empty. However, on the occasions when I have experienced true detachment, I am stunned by the amazing peace that accompanies it.

Don't be mistaken—detachment goes against all natural inclinations. That's why it's something that we have to ask God to give us. But it is something God wants us to experience. God wants it so much that he guarantees that he will give it to us if we ask.

However, we first have to ask for it—and "there's the rub." When we ask for detachment, we are allowed to tell God our preferences, but we don't get to request a specific outcome. Detachment means that we don't presume to advise God and that we trust him completely to do what is best.

That's one more little thing about the prayers God can't refuse to answer. We have to trust completely—not wavering in our belief—that God is going to do the right thing by us. That's what detachment really means: the complete confidence that, in the words of Julian of Norwich, "all shall be well, and all shall be well, and all manner of thing shall be well."

The fact is that most of us don't really want to experience detachment. We don't want to trust God with the outcome, because we aren't totally convinced that he knows what's best for us. We feel the need to tell him, sometimes in great detail, just how we think things should be. We act as if we have the right to be God's advisors, particularly when it comes to our own lives, because deep down we just don't trust him.

Does God Know about My Bills?

Unless you trust with every fiber of your being that God will do what is best for you, then you can't be detached about the outcome. Believe me, it isn't easy. My particular temptation is to worry about my financial future. I have a horror of living under a bridge with my few possessions in a shopping cart. In my dread, I'm pretty sure that I'm barefoot and that my cat is starving, as well.

Therein lies the heart of detachment. As the prayer says, we ask for it so that we might love God's holy will. But what if God's holy will turns out to be something really unpleasant? What if God wants something I really don't want, something I dread? What if God's will for me means trying to find a wireless Internet connection for my laptop as I push my shopping cart under a bridge? Most of us struggle with the concept of

God's will at least some of the time. One of the reasons may be that we've been told over and over to pray, "Your will, not mine." After all, that's what Jesus prayed just before his death. If most of us were totally honest, we don't like to pray those words. When we pray "Your will, not mine," it usually means that something very unpleasant is happening to us, and we are trying to feel pious about it. We are expecting the worst, but we don't want to think that God is going to do a number on us, so we say, "Your will, not mine." What we would really rather do is kick and scream at God and try to force him to be nicer to us. Saying "your will" is a way to bury our frustration and shove the anger we are feeling at God back into a pious box.

We may also secretly believe that every time we add "Your will, not mine" to a request, God is going to give us a big fat NO for an answer. It's not surprising that we think this way. The one time we know for sure that Jesus got no for an answer was in the Garden of Gethsemane, when he asked that the cup be removed from him and said—you guessed it—"Your will, not mine." When we ask God for something, and we're pretty sure we're not going to get it, we add, "Your will, not mine," to keep from being disappointed. It's really a way of saying, "You aren't going to give it to me anyway, so I guess it must be your will, and I'm going to pretend that I like it."

Another reason we say "Your will be done" is that we get the cockeyed notion that God doesn't want us to be happy; so we try to use "reverse psychology" on God. We have the wild idea that if we can somehow trick him into thinking we want the thing we really don't want, then maybe he'll give us the thing we do want. It won't work, but that doesn't keep us from trying.

Which brings us to Gethsemane. Didn't Jesus get no for an answer when he prayed before his death? Well, sort of. Remember that Jesus had already agreed to die. He had willingly accepted the cross. If he had changed his mind that last night, he didn't need to spend long hours literally sweating blood, begging the Father for a miracle rescue. Instead of leaving the Passover meal and walking to the Garden of Gethsemane with his friends, he could have packed a bag with leftovers, headed for the gates to the city, and set out into the desert. There he could have met up with the next caravan and gone to Egypt or Persia or a hundred other places where he would have been out of reach of both Jewish and Roman authority. Instead he prayed in the garden, as he waited for Judas and the cohort to arrive.

When the Answer Is No

When Jesus asked that the cup be removed, he wasn't giving us an example of how to take no for answer, as we so often think. He already knew that the answer had to be no. Instead, he was revealing that, like us, he was fully human, with all the fears and panic that come packaged in our strands of DNA. He was letting us know that when we are deeply fearful about our future, God knows exactly what those feelings are like. He was showing us that with God's help, we, too, can overcome our natural fears and fulfill God's will for our lives.

That night Jesus was doing what we all do—begging God for something when what we really know we need is God's grace to endure it. Jesus prayed that prayer in the garden because he was our brother, like us in everything save sin.

Jesus' example shows us that overcoming our fears and becoming detached aren't things we can do on our own. They require grace—an infusion of God's own strength and insight. Even Jesus needed it. That's why we need it. If it were part of our natural makeup, we wouldn't struggle so. We would just detach without conscious thought.

Asking for God's Love

Yeah, okay, enough intellectualizing. What do you *do* to gain detachment?

It's deceptively easy: you ask for a share of God's love.

When we ask to experience God's love, we can be absolutely positive that we will receive it. That's one of the gifts God has to give us. No matter what we have done in our past, no matter how little our faith, when we ask for a share of God's love, God will give it to us.

As God's love enters our hearts and minds, the first sign is a sense of peace. Now you might not go from panic to peace in an instant (although you could). Instead, you may just sense a little lessening of the grip of fear, a brief respite in which you can see and appreciate the goodness around you and momentarily forget your problems.

As you go deeper into God's love, you may feel a certain ripple of confidence that all is unfolding according to plan—a plan that you might not understand, but that you know exists. You have a sense you can't explain that "everything is okay."

Finally, when you are completely surrounded by God's love, you experience a sense of release of the situation into God's hands. You simply know that whatever happens, it will be fine. You don't need reassurance from anyone. You know in a place beyond knowing that "all shall be well."

When you enter that place, you are beginning to experience the "self-detachment" that allows you to love God's will, no matter what it is. You no longer cling to your own desires but know that whatever happens comes from a God who loves you and wants only the best for you. God's holy will becomes your greatest desire.

I don't want to give you the impression that this is easy. It isn't. In fact, it is impossible to do it alone. Which leads us to the next grace.

Oh, and the job?

I didn't get it.

But that's ok. The right person did.

CHAPTER SIX

Confidence in Confidence

Fourth, grant me the grace to have confidence in the merits of Jesus Christ and in the intercession of Mary [and the saints].

In *The Sound of Music*, Maria expresses her fears and inadequacies as she leaves the convent to become governess to Captain von Trapp's seven children. At the end of her song, she sings that her confidence isn't found in numbers or wealth, but "confidence in confidence alone."

When I was younger, I thought that was a rather odd thing to say. How can you have confidence in confidence? Now, a bit older and (I hope) wiser, I am beginning to understand what Rodgers and Hammerstein—and by extension, Maria—meant.

When you put your trust in circumstances, things, or even people, you may be disappointed. Objects deteriorate, people may let you down, the world changes. It's only when you look within yourself, in that place where you are intimately united with God, that you can even hope to have confidence that you are making right choices. Only God can give you the courage to become the person he wants you to be.

It is there, in the deepest part of our being where we unite with Jesus, that we find our ability to have confidence. We don't find it in something that is transitory, but in God himself.

So let's talk a little about confidence, what it is and what it isn't, and how it relates to the five graces.

No Guarantee, No Warranty

First off, confidence isn't the same as a guarantee. You can't have confidence in something you know without a doubt to be true. For instance, you don't have confidence that you were born. You know you were born, because you are sitting here reading these words. You can have confidence that you were born on a certain day to certain parents, because it's always possible that you were born on a different day or to different parents. It may be highly unlikely, but the possibility still exists. So you can be confident that the people you call Mom and Dad are your parents and that the day on your birth certificate is really the day you entered the world, but you don't have confidence in the fact you actually were born. You *know* that you were born.

Another thing confidence isn't: a positive feeling. Many people mistake an emotion for confidence. They say, "I feel confident that I'm going to win the lottery!" Or "I feel confident that I'm going to lose weight." They are caught up in the emotion of the moment and convince themselves that their optimism is the same thing as confidence. I've even had people who are Jehovah's Witnesses come to my door and try to convince me that their additional books of sacred text are inspired by God by referring to emotion as confidence. "Read with an open mind," they tell me, "and see if your heart does not burn within you. If it does, then you can have confidence that what you read is true." Obviously that doesn't work. If nice personal feelings were the criteria for determining the validity of Scripture, *The Adventures of Tom Sawyer* would be in the canon because I get a warm feeling inside whenever I read it. Emotions and confidence are two different things, and never the twain shall meet.

Confidence is a combination of certainty and hope. It's the deep-seated conviction that even though we may not yet know the results, we trust they will come to pass. Confidence really is "the substance of things to be hoped for, the evidence of things that appear not," as the Douay-Rheims version of Hebrews 11:1 tells us. We believe, even though we do not see. We trust, even though we may have doubts. Confidence is, in fact, very closely related to faith.

But that's getting a bit ahead of ourselves. For now, the question is, what can we trust?

In God We Trust

The answer is not a "what" but "who."

I have a friend who is a very devout Hindu. We talk often about the spiritual life, and while we agree on some things, we vehemently disagree on one foundational point. He believes that in order to communicate with God, we first need to find a spiritual master, a guru, through whom we can reach God and through whom God can reach us.

"How do you know you are talking to God if you don't have a guru to tell you?" he asks me.

"How do you know you are talking to God just because the guru tells you?" I ask back.

"You can't trust yourself to know if it is God speaking or your own mind," he replies.

"So how can you believe that the guru knows it's God and not his own mind giving advice?" I respond.

As you might suspect, our discussions often end at this point. As a Christian, I don't need a spiritual master to tell me I'm communicating with God. That's because, in a certain sense, I have the only true "guru" possible. It's just that my "guru" isn't a mere man. He is Jesus himself. Through Jesus I can communicate directly with God, because Jesus is the second Person of the Trinity. I don't begin to understand the mysteries behind the incarnation, but I do know that as a Christian, my path to the Father lies in the example, the teaching, and the merits of Jesus.

Having someone you can see and hear tell you what to do and believe may seem easier than putting your trust in Jesus, who can be seen and heard only with the eyes and ears of faith. However, a human being, no matter how holy, can never be more than a fallible human being. He or she cannot define our relationship with God for us, and she or he certainly cannot live it for us. We must build and live that relationship for ourselves. That's why the fourth request asks that we be given the grace to place our confidence, our trust and belief, in the merits of Jesus.

The Merits of Jesus

By asking to have confidence in the merits of Jesus, we are actually asking for the gift of faith. We have to have faith that Jesus is who he says he is in order for us to believe that what he did has validity for our lives. That's what having confidence in his merits means. Jesus shows us the way to the Father, the way to live, the way to love. He said he is "the way and the truth and the life" (John 14:6). If we do not have faith in him, then we cannot have confidence that what he has told us and shown us is the right way to live. We must ask for faith so that we might believe . . . and we believe so that we might live.

According to St. Paul, as he explains in his various letters to the churches of Asia Minor, faith has three main components. First, it is our desire to be in right union with God—what we ask for in the first grace. Second, it is submission of our will to the will of God—what we request in the third grace. Finally, faith is trust in Jesus as our brother and savior—exactly what we ask for in this fourth grace.

Sometimes those of us who have been in the church all or most of our lives forget that faith is a gift. I know people who want to believe, but who do not have the gift of faith. I don't claim to have any special knowledge of why certain people lack faith, but I suspect that one reason is that they haven't asked for it. Perhaps they've said the words, even said them aloud in a church, but they haven't asked with their whole being. They want to know what faith is like, but they aren't sure they really want to have it.

Even when you have the gift of faith, however, there will be times when you have doubts or question God. Even saints like Blessed Mother Teresa of Calcutta are said to have had moments of doubt. What having faith means is that you are open and receptive to God's actions in your life. You are willing to step out in prayer, expecting an answer. You are willing to allow God to share your life. It means that you will try, to the best of your ability, to unite your life with God's purposes for you. You may still question, you may still doubt, but you will never be able to completely deny. That's what the gift of faith does. It removes the option to honestly deny the existence of God. Once you have faith, you will always know that you must accept him or not, live for him or not. God is a reality.

Intercede for Me!

Along with the gift of faith through the merits of Jesus, God has another gift he desires to give us—the love and assistance of Mary and the saints.

I am positively convinced that Mary and the saints intercede for us, just as this grace says. Let me tell you about one time when I experienced an intercession that to this day still amazes me.

I was driving alone on a dark, two-lane country road in a blinding rainstorm. My wipers barely cleared the windshield long enough for me to glimpse the next few feet ahead. I considered pulling over and stopping, but without a shoulder on the road, I was afraid someone would plow into me from behind. I just crept along, praying that St. Dominic, a saint to whom I have particular devotion, would help me.

Suddenly I felt a horrendous crunch. The car lurched forward and rocked to a sudden stop. I couldn't tell what had happened, so I opened the door to get out and immediately fell into a deep puddle of mud. When I picked myself up, I was soaked to the skin, but that was the least of my problems. My car was perched on top of a concrete divider that had been placed in the road as a detour. In the blinding rain, I hadn't been able to see it and had driven up onto it. Now my car was completely stuck, all four wheels dangling about a foot off the ground.

Bear in mind, I had been to a party at a country estate, so I was wearing spike heels and a flimsy party dress—not exactly suitable for hiking along country roads on a cold, dark, rainy night. This was well before cell phones became ubiquitous, too, so I was literally stranded.

I crawled back in the car, turned on the flashers, and waited. The minutes turned into an hour. I was growing chilled, and the prospect of spending the night was getting more and more probable since not a single car had gone by. I also was getting scared. Finally I decided I had to do something. I got out of the car again and promptly lost heart. There simply was no way to get the car off the divider without a tow truck. Even then, the undercarriage was going to be badly damaged because I could see the deep scratches in the concrete where I had traveled several feet on the divider. I was in real trouble.

Climbing back in the car, I dropped my head on the steering wheel and said quietly, "Help me, St. Dominic." Then, without any logical reason whatsoever, I turned on the ignition and pressed the gas. I felt the car rise slightly and move sideways, landing with a bump. I looked out the passenger window and saw that the car was completely off the divider and resting in the middle of the highway. Cautiously, I applied a little more gas. The car worked fine, and I drove home without any mishaps.

In the morning, I took the car in to the shop, explaining that I had been in an accident the night before and was afraid the underside was damaged. The mechanic crawled under my car, examined it, and came out with a puzzled expression. "There's nothing wrong," he said. "There aren't even any scratches."

All I could think of at that moment was "Thank you, St. Dominic!"

The truth is, we aren't alone in this life. We have Mary and all the saints to assist us. This grace reminds us that when we are in need, no matter what the need is, all we have to do is ask for help.

The assistance might not be as dramatic or as miraculous as lifting a car off a divider. In my case, I might have been aided by someone coming along the road or by being kept safe until morning. Those would have been answers to prayer, too. I received aid in a way I never anticipated and still find hard to believe, but I do know that I was given the help I needed exactly when I needed it most.

God will always give us the gift of the intercession of Mary and the saints. We can have complete confidence that God will come to our aid—even if we don't always know what that assistance will look like. We don't always ask for his help, however. All too often we think we can handle whatever life flings our way all by ourselves.

Which brings us to the last of the five graces.

CHAPTER SEVEN

Keep On Keeping On

Fifth, I ask for the grace of perseverance, knowing that whenever I call on you for assistance, you will answer my call and come to my aid.

Pick up any magazine at the checkout stand of your local supermarket, and you can read the "motivational story of the week." Woman climbs Mt. Everest blindfolded! Couple loses fortune and rebuilds it by recycling Popsicle sticks! Woman loses three hundred pounds by eating only broccoli soup for three years! I'm exaggerating a little, but you get the idea. While the details of the stories vary, the one thing they all have in common is the protagonist's perseverance. The people who don't give up are the ones who ultimately succeed.

We know this. We know that in order to achieve any goal, we have to carry through to the end. It's not enough to come off the blocks; we have to persevere to the finish line. However, it doesn't come as a surprise that many of us struggle with perseverance. We have trouble sticking to something until it is completed. We know we should exercise more self-discipline and willpower, but somewhere along the way, we quit. We give up, often within sight of our goal.

But that's not the worst of it. Not only do we give up, we then beat ourselves up for being a failure, which sets us up for even more failure in the future.

"Almost" Doesn't Cut It

I know all too well how this works. Once upon a time, I decided that I would get down to the weight I was in high school. I began a strict diet and exercise program and lost nearly twenty-five pounds. My self-esteem soared, and as the pounds came off, I felt like I could do anything. For six months, I persevered.

Did you notice that I said I lost "nearly" twenty-five pounds? Well, there's the stickler. I quit with two pounds to go. I told myself that I'd almost made it. I convinced myself that I was so close that it really was the same thing. I assured myself that no one would know but me.

What happened next isn't something I like to admit. Because I didn't persevere to the end, it became very easy to say that three pounds over the goal was virtually the same as two. Then five, then ten. Within a few months, I had gained back all the weight I had lost.

Since then, I've struggled with weight issues because I failed once, and now I think that I'll always fail—all because I didn't persevere to the final goal the first time.

I don't share this story to gain your sympathy, but to point out that perseverance isn't something we can do on our own. We need the fifth grace.

We don't ask for this grace just to have perseverance for perseverance's sake alone. Doggedly keeping on is hardly a virtue. The reason for perseverance comes back to trust. We ask for this grace so that we can trust that God will answer us when we call for aid. We need it because prayer doesn't work like a divine vending machine. We can't just drop in a few Hail Marys and a couple of Our Fathers and automatically get results. More often than not, we have to keep asking; we have to persevere.

Perseverance in Prayer

The concept of perseverance in prayer is so important that Jesus addresses it several times. Unfortunately, he does so in parables, which can be a bit confusing. Take, for instance, the story of the woman before the wicked judge. Jesus begins by talking about "the necessity for them to pray always without becoming weary":

"There was a judge in a certain town who neither feared God nor respected any human being. And a widow in that town used to come to him and say, 'Render a just decision for me against my adversary.' For a long time the judge was unwilling, but eventually he thought, 'While it is true that I neither fear God nor respect any human being, because this widow keeps bothering me I shall deliver a just decision for her lest she finally come and strike me.'" The Lord said, "Pay attention to what the dishonest judge says. Will not God then secure the rights of his chosen ones who call out to him day and night? Will he be slow to answer them? I tell you, he will see to it that justice is done for them speedily." (Luke 18:1-8)

At first read, Jesus seems to be saying that we need to nag God before he will answer our prayer, just as the judge had to be nagged by the widow before she obtained a verdict. However, that's not really what Jesus was saying. His point was that if a bad man will answer a persistent plea, how much more so will God, who loves us, answer our persistent prayers? The parable is meant to encourage us to not give up when our prayers don't appear to be answered, but to continue praying in confidence that God will answer at the exact right time.

This concept is so important that Jesus shares yet another parable about the need to persist:

And he said to them, "Suppose one of you has a friend to whom he goes at midnight and says, 'Friend, lend me three loaves of bread, for a friend of mine has arrived at my house from a journey and I have nothing to offer him,' and he says in reply from within, 'Do not bother me; the door has already been locked and my children and I are already in bed. I cannot get up to give you anything.' I tell you, if he does not get up to give him the loaves because of their friendship, he will get up to give him whatever he needs because of his persistence.

"And I tell you, ask and you will receive; seek and you will find; knock and the door will be opened to you. For everyone who asks, receives; and the one who seeks, finds; and to the one who knocks, the door will be opened. What father among you would hand his son a snake when he asks for a fish? Or hand him a scorpion when he asks for an egg? If you then, who are wicked, know how to give good gifts to your children, how much more will the Father in heaven give the holy Spirit to those who ask him?" (Luke 11:5-13)

Again, Jesus isn't telling us that God has to be badgered into answering us, but he is trying to encourage us to have faith that God will always answer if we have the strength and courage to keep our hearts and minds focused on our request. In other words, we will get our prayers answered as long as we unwaveringly trust in God's promise to answer them.

Why? The Big Question

Why doesn't God answer our prayers right away? Why is it necessary that we keep on asking over and over again?

That question has puzzled philosophers and theologians, and I do not presume to have the definitive answer. But I do know that in my own life, persistence in prayer has resulted in changes in me even when the circumstances themselves haven't changed.

For many years, I wanted a relationship that was unhealthy and damaged to be healed. Not a day went by that I didn't ask God for healing. I made more novenas, said more rosaries, and asked more people to pray for me than I can remember. All I wanted was for this damaged relationship to be made whole.

As the years went on, I grew more and more puzzled. Why would God refuse what seemed to me to be a good and honorable request? So I kept praying, and the relationship continued to deteriorate, until finally, it simply ended.

I was devastated. How could this have happened? Didn't I ask, seek, and knock? Didn't I persist? It felt very much like God was handing me a scorpion instead of an egg.

When it became apparent that the relationship was never going to be what I prayed for, I grew angry with God. To be honest, I was furious at God. For some time, I didn't want to talk to God at all, especially not about this situation. If you had asked me about it right then, I would probably have told you that I thought God was a liar who didn't keep his promises.

That was, of course, my emotional reaction. Eventually, because God is patient and understanding, I came back, this time asking God to help me understand what had happened. Gradually, I began to realize that my prayers had changed the relationship, and healing had occurred. Just not the way I had expected.

The fact is that I had changed. I was no longer willing to accept the unhealthy dynamics that the relationship was predicated on. I had gradually become healthier through those years of prayer but, for whatever reason, the other person hadn't, so the relationship could not continue. I had asked for healing, and I was given healing. I was healed of the need to cling to a relationship that was spiritually, mentally, and emotionally damaging. The changes had been so gradual over those long years of prayer that it wasn't until the relationship was over that I could see how God actually had been answering my prayer all along. Thank God I had persisted long enough to recognize it.

"Spiritual 911"

Ultimately, I like to think of this fifth grace as a sort of "Spiritual 911." When we call 911, we expect that help will come. When we ask for this grace, we are asking for the ability to believe that whenever we call upon God for assistance, God will come to our aid. Just as we know that the police or fire department will come when we call, even before we hear the sirens, so, too, we need to believe that God will come to our aid, will answer us, even when we don't yet see the answer.

So how does God come to our aid? Sometimes we get a miracle, like the miraculous assistance I got when my car was stuck on the divider; but most of the time, God's assistance comes to us through other people. And much of the time, the aid comes in a form we aren't anticipating.

A modern parable illustrates this in an amusing fashion: A river flooded, and a man was trapped on the roof of his house. He prayed that God would rescue him. As he was waiting, a man came by in a rowboat and told him to get in. The trapped man declined the offer, saying that God was going to rescue him. A few hours later, a search and rescue boat approached. Again the man told his would-be rescuers that he didn't need them, because God was going to save him. Finally, as night was falling, a police helicopter hovered overhead. Again the man refused rescue, saying that God was coming for him. Sometime in the night, the water rose and the man drowned. When he entered heaven, he approached God and said, "I prayed and prayed that you would rescue me. Why didn't you answer me?" "What do you mean?" God answered, "I sent a rowboat, I sent a rescue boat, and I sent a helicopter. What more were you expecting?"

As amusing as this story is, it reminds us that as we pray in our hour of need, we must remain open to the answers God sends us—which may or may not come in the form we are imagining.

We May Be God's Answer

Finally, we must also remember that not only does God's aid come to us through other people, we are also meant to be God's aid to other people.

The five graces aren't just about what we get from God; they are also about what we give to others in God's name. When we feel an inner prompting that nudges us out of our complacency, we need to pay attention. It might be as simple as taking a few minutes to thank the grocery clerk for packing your bags carefully or it might be as complex as figuring out a way to get potable water to a village in Africa. The size or difficulty of the task isn't what's important. What is important is that we remember the words of St. Teresa of Ávila:

Christ has no body now on earth but yours,
  no hands but yours,
  no feet but yours,
Yours are the eyes through which he looks with
  compassion on the world
Yours are the feet with which he is to go about
  doing good;
Yours are the hands with which he is to bless men now.

Whose prayer might *you* be the answer to today?

Daily Bread

The first time I made bread, I didn't realize that because there were no preservatives in it, the bread would rapidly mold if left unrefrigerated. When I saw the blue-green spores, I suddenly understood what the words "Give us our daily bread" in the Our Father meant. Homemade bread isn't something you can store for days and weeks in advance. It has to be made fresh and used each and every day.

The same thing holds true for perseverance. You can't stock up on it. You have to ask for it and use it daily, sometimes several times a day. It truly is spiritual "daily bread."

Of all the gifts God wants to give us, the gift of perseverance is the one I treasure the most. Perhaps it's because I know all too well that I lack any semblance of the virtue on my own. The great irony of it is that I have to persevere in asking for perseverance.

We all do.

Every day.

Chapter Eight

In My Hour of Need

I fear only that I will neglect to turn to you in time of need, and thus bring myself to ruin.

Before we can accept the gifts God wants to give us, we still have to examine the one thing we are afraid to admit: we are afraid.

We are afraid that nothing we believe about God is true. We are afraid that our prayers won't be answered. We are afraid that we really arc all alone, and the only thing that awaits us is oblivion.

It's primal fear, the fear as old as time itself.

When our pulse begins to race and our blood pressure rises, we need to take a deep breath and realize that God tells us that the only thing we have to fear is that we will not allow him to help us.

Like "the more we give, the more we have," this is one of those paradoxes we encounter as we grow more deeply in the spiritual life. Even though our deepest fear is that there is no God who loves us, the only antidote to our fear is to trust that the God who loves us will be there.

This isn't something that we can work out with logic. We can't run a spreadsheet or create a list of pros and cons that will convince us. All we can do it take the proverbial leap of faith. At some point, we either have to lower the barriers of our fear and let God in, or keep them up and let the fear increase until it destroys us. It's the only choice we've got.

Ruination

What happens if we cling to our fears?

We will bring ourselves to ruin. That's not a threat; it's just a statement of reality. When we neglect to turn to God in our hour of need, it isn't God who forces ruin upon us. We bring the ruin upon ourselves. Sometimes it's easy to see how we bring ourselves to ruin. We do things that we know aren't right, but we somehow believe we will be spared the consequences. We smoke, thinking we won't get lung cancer. We drink and drive, believing we will be lucky enough to avoid an accident. We lie, cheat, manipulate—all the while trying to convince ourselves that we will be able to avoid the negative fallout of our choices. Deep down, however, we know that we have only ourselves to blame when the consequences catch up with us.

Another kind of ruin is much more subtle. This is the ruin that comes from making choices that seem good, but aren't really

God's will for us. Because we either don't bother or aren't willing to seek divine guidance, we can easily end up making decisions that are detrimental to our long-term spiritual well-being. The lure, the trap, is that because we are relying solely on our human logic, we believe we are making a good choice. In fact, we may think we are making the only correct choice.

Take, for example, a family where all the children are expected to go to college, get a degree, and become a professional. Nothing wrong with that. Having a good education and a sound career is one of the things all parents want for their children.

But what if one of the children doesn't want to become an attorney or an accountant or an engineer? What if she wants to be a police officer? What if God has given her the burning desire to "catch bad guys" and take care of the innocent? What if she would be an excellent police officer, but instead, she does what seems to be the "right" thing and becomes an accountant? The reality is that if God planted the desire in her heart to be a police officer because that was his will for her—that was how she could give God the greatest glory in her life—then I can almost guarantee you that no matter how much professional success she has, she will never be completely satisfied with her life. Some part of her will always be at odds with her choice. This doesn't mean that her life can't be blessed or she can't be happy doing taxes instead of catching criminals; and she can still find ways to give glory to God in her life, because God redeems all our choices, even those we haven't prayed through. But it does mean that her life will have challenges that God never intended her to face.

Can I Have a Neon Sign?

I've often wished that God would reveal his plan for the stages of my life with a neon sign. If that isn't possible, maybe a lengthy letter with a detailed to-do list. Alas, God doesn't seem inclined to offer me guidance the way I want. So I have to accept his direction in the ways he deems suitable.

Often those directions come in the form of inner promptings, "coincidences" that aren't really coincidental at all—the convergence of people and events that simply can't be ignored or doors that close tightly and bar my path.

I majored in advertising and marketing in college. While I was in school, I realized that I didn't care for advertising and I really didn't like copywriting. But I was so far into the program that it seemed like a waste not to continue, so I finished. Newly married, with my degree in hand and in need of a job, I accepted the first offer that was made to me, to be a copywriter at an up-and-coming ad agency.

From the very beginning, I didn't fit. I didn't share the values of my colleagues or their lifestyles, but I ignored all the inner promptings that were encouraging me to find something else. One day my boss came to me with a "volunteer" project—the kind of "volunteer" project that you can't turn down. He wanted me to become a consultant for the local Planned Parenthood office and help them write their ads. With a sinking heart, I told him that I couldn't, in good conscience, write ads that advocated abortion. He nodded and walked out of my office. Shortly thereafter I was fired for incompetence.

I can still remember cleaning out my desk in shock and mortification. The week before I was fired, I had gotten a raise, and now, all of a sudden, I was incompetent? At that time in my life, I was a Sunday Christian at best. I attended church, but didn't spend any time in prayer or reflection about my life, so my first reaction was to get angry at God. Why did he allow me to be fired? When my anger subsided, I was disappointed that God hadn't been "nicer" to me, since after all, I had refused to write ads for abortion.

If I had known St. Teresa of Ávila's donkey story at the time, I probably would have had her words made into a poster. According to the legend, St. Teresa was crossing a rain-swollen river on a donkey cart. The donkey balked, as donkeys often do, at entering the turbid water. Teresa and the sisters who were with her tried to force the issue, and ended up wet, muddy, and cold. In frustration, Teresa is said to have looked up to heaven and commented, "God, if this is the way you treat your friends, no wonder you have so few of them!" I would have fully understood her annoyance. At the time, I didn't think that God was being very friendly to me, either.

Years later, I encountered some of the people I had worked with and saw the direction their lives had taken. It was then I realized that I had been too blind and too stubborn to pay attention to the clues God had sent to me, so he had to do something drastic to remove me from the path I was determined to walk. Had I continued doing what I was doing, I am quite sure that my life would have taken me further and further from God's will.

Once I realized that God was blessing me by having me fired, I made up my mind that I would never again seek a full-time job in advertising. I've done a few freelance projects now and then, but I have trusted that God doesn't want me in that line of work and that he will provide other streams of income. So far, for more than twenty years, he has done just that. Even in my moments of fear—and I still have them—I remind myself that God really does know about mortgage payments and electric bills. He is trustworthy, but I'm the one who needs to do the trusting.

Course Correction

"Oh great," you may be thinking. "It's way too late for me to become the (fill in the blank) I should have been. Now I'm stuck."

No, that's the wonderful, amazing thing about God. He exists outside of our limits of time and space, so there is always time for a course correction. Now because we do live in time and space, we don't get a complete makeover. If you are fifty with bad knees, you aren't going to be able to become the ballet dancer you might have been. However, with God's help, you can still find a way to utilize the talents that you have let go fallow. Perhaps you will be able to work with a local ballet company in staging performances. Or help choreograph a ballet. Or just go with your grandchildren to their dance classes and encourage them. If you have been called to do something with your life, it's never too late to do it. God doesn't put a time limit on his gifts to you, and neither should you. So pay attention to the voice of the Spirit within, who is the true compass who will never mislead you.

Time of Need

It should be clear by now that our times of need aren't those moments of crisis we all face at some point in our lives. When we are in a literal or figurative foxhole, we become acutely aware of our need. Most times, when things are going well, we tend to forget about consulting God and begin to assume that we can handle our lives by ourselves. We may even think that we shouldn't be bothering God about the small things; instead, we will wait until something major crops up.

The difficulty is that if we wait for the big things, we never build the confidence we need to truly trust God. Every day, every hour of every day, we are in need of God's guidance. When we learn to ask and accept guidance in small decisions, then it's much easier to ask and accept guidance in big, critical ones.

Of all the lessons that Jesus taught us about being in relationship with the Father, this one may be near the top in importance. Jesus depended on the Father for everything in his life, reminding us that if the Father knows when a sparrow falls, how much more does he know when we are in need. Because Jesus was in the habit of relying on God, he was able to trust (that word again) when it came time for the ultimate sacrifice of his life. He had a foundation built on a lifetime of asking for and receiving aid from the Father. His entire life was one of constant, continual dialogue with God. We are called to have that same kind of relationship with the Father. That's why there is one more important and final grace that we must ask for—the grace to be able to pray always.

CHAPTER NINE

To Pray Constantly

Grant me the grace to pray always.

When I first heard we should pray always, I was probably in fourth grade at St. Anthony's grade school in Missoula, Montana. I distinctly remember my reaction; I figured that meant I had to stop playing with my Barbie dolls, never romp with my dog, and spend the entire rest of my life saying the rosary. Since I didn't like praying the rosary, the whole prospect was not very enticing. However, being a dutiful and devout child, that Lent I took Sister's well-meaning admonition to heart and gave up every single recess to say the rosary in the darkened church.

I think that was one of the main reasons I concluded that I did not have a religious vocation and was adamant on Vocations Day that I was not taking any habit, ever. In fact, I think that experience tainted my notion of continual prayer for the next twenty years. It didn't do much for my appreciation of the rosary, either.

What Prayer Isn't

Gradually I began to reframe my idea of what constitutes prayer. It doesn't mean kneeling in a church, repeating Hail Marys until your mind goes blank and the beads fall from your numb fingers. To pray always means to have your whole being—heart, mind, and strength—oriented in a "Godward" direction.

It's just that simple. It doesn't mean you neglect your duties or abandon your relationships or ignore your own physical needs. It simply means that you allow God access to every moment of your life.

All too often we think that prayer must entail words, but Brother Lawrence prayed in the midst of the pots and pans: "Nor is it needful that we should have great things to do. . . . We can do little things for God; I turn the cake that is frying on the pan for love of him, and that done, if there is nothing else to call me, I prostrate myself in worship before him, who has given me grace to work; afterwards I rise happier than a king. It is enough for me to pick up but a straw from the ground for the love of God" (*The Practice of the Presence of God*).

The idea behind praying always is to turn all time into prayer. Setting aside time for saying specific words is good, but it's better to make your being into the words and your entire life into the prayer. As St. Thérèse of Lisieux says, "For me, *prayer* is an aspiration of the heart, it is a simple glance directed to heaven, it is a cry of gratitude and love in the midst of trial as well as joy" (*Story of a Soul*).

Of course, the saints make it sound so easy. That's probably why they are saints and we aren't. So how do we start this process of making our lives into continual prayer?

The Power of the Word

We begin by realizing that thoughts and words have untold power. Everything that exists began first as a thought, a word, as it were. The Wright brothers thought about flying, imagining what it would be to take flight, and through the power of their thoughts turned into action, modern airplanes came into being.

The creative process of the word began with God. God created the world with words through the power of the Word. "In the beginning was the Word, and the Word was with God, and the Word was God. He was in the beginning with God. All things came to be through him, and without him nothing came to be. What came to be through him was life, and this life was the light of the human race" (John 1:1-4).

Everything has come into being through God's words and the Word. Because we are made in God's image and likeness, our words also have enormous power for both good and bad. Because the words we think have such a great effect on what happens in our lives, the first place where we learn to pray always is by exercising discipline over the words we think.

We will attract into our lives the things we think and talk about. It's almost as if our thoughts are a magnet. Like a magnet, we draw like to like. In other words, if our thoughts focus on the positive and are filled with gratitude, we will draw to us positive things for which to be grateful. If our thoughts are constantly centered on the negative, we will have more things to be negative about.

We really will have in our lives what we expect. Consider for a moment what it's like being in the presence of someone who constantly finds fault with everything and everybody. It's almost as if they are surrounded by an aura of negativity, something like the dirt cloud that hung over the head of Pigpen in the old *Peanuts* comic strip. In fact, negativity becomes a self-fulfilling prophecy. The more negative people are, the more negative things seem to happen to them.

The opposite is also true. I have a friend who continually reminds me to "take every thought captive," quoting 2 Corinthians 10:5. When she catches me saying things like, "I can't do that," she gently points out that as long as I talk about not being able to do something, that's probably what is going to happen. With her encouragement, I've begun to train myself to say things like, "I am recovering from this cold," instead of "I'm as sick as a dog," and "My day is getting better," instead of "What a lousy day I'm having." Sometimes it can feel like you are denying reality when you are on your fifth box of tissues and yet another obstacle has entered your path, but by putting your attention on what you want—even if it's not yet here—you shift your entire being—body and soul—into a place where what you want to happen can begin to happen. When you say that you are recovering from the cold even as you are sneezing, you stimulate your immune system, you take your mind off your miserable symptoms, and you begin to believe that you really are going to get better soon.

It's a bit like the "little engine that could" in the children's story. As the little train pulled an impossible load up the hill, he kept telling himself, "I think I can, I think I can," and he can—and does. Had he been telling himself, "I know I can't, I know I can't," he never would have accomplished his task. By thinking positive thoughts, even in a negative situation, you find strength you never knew you had. What's more, I've learned through trial and error that turning my thoughts and words toward the good that is always present shifts my consciousness into a state of gratitude—and gratitude in and of itself is a form of prayer.

Admittedly, words alone can't stop bad things from happening to us. But which patient do you think gets the most support from a doctor? One who says, "I'm going to do all that I can to get better" or one who says, "I'm giving up; I'm going to die anyway"?

So, the first step in turning our lives into prayer is to make sure that the words we think and the words we speak are oriented toward the good, the positive, the creative, the hopeful. We have much more power than we can imagine when we live our words and the Word lives in us. We truly become what we think. We truly have the ability to shape our lives into a reflection of God's love and glory by the way we think and speak.

One of my favorite stories exemplifies this truth. A man was walking on the beach where he lived when he met a woman coming from the opposite direction. The woman stopped him and said she was thinking about moving to his town. She asked him what kind of people lived there. In turn, he asked her what kind of people lived in the town she was leaving. "Oh," she said, "they are selfish, unkind, rude, and very unpleasant. That's why I want to move." He told her that, unfortunately, she would probably find the people in this town to be exactly the same way—selfish, unkind, rude, and very unpleasant.

A little later, on the same beach, he met another woman who was also thinking about moving to his town. She, too, asked him what the people were like, and he asked her what the people were like in the town she was currently living in. "They are just wonderful," she said. "Kind, considerate, generous, loving. I can hardly bear to think about leaving them." The man smiled, and told her not to worry because she would probably find the people in the new town to be exactly the same as the ones she was leaving—kind, considerate, generous, and loving.

The point is, of course, that we most often find what we expect to find. When we expect bad, we will probably find it. When we expect to find good, we will. I had always heard that the French were very rude to Americans, but because I have several close French friends, I never allowed that thought to be part of my reality. When my son was a teenager, we were traveling in the South of France when he became very ill and was hospitalized. I was naturally very concerned about him, and because I didn't speak much French at the time, I blundered terribly in my attempts to communicate. However, I tried my best to be as polite and as respectful as possible. I can honestly say that because I was not expecting to encounter rudeness, I never did. The small town we were in had only a few taxis, and by the end of our stay, the cabbies who took me to and from the hospital were asking how "the young American" was, often cutting their fees because I had used their services so often. The owner of the small hotel I was staying in even began driving me to the hospital in his car so that I wouldn't have to pay the cab fares! Despite the stress, I experienced profound love and goodness all around me. (My son recovered and was eventually sent home to have surgery, by the way.)

That experience was not unique. I can honestly say that nowhere in the world where I have ventured have I ever been treated rudely. But then, I never allow thoughts of rudeness to come into my mind, and I work very hard not to be a rude American myself. I firmly believe that positive things have always happened to me because I do my best to focus on the positives, not the negatives.

Present in the Present

If the first step in praying constantly is to focus our energy and thoughts, the next step is to be present in the present. Multi-tasking is a modern-day virtue, but being able to text on your cell phone while surfing the Internet on your computer and watching the TV all the while you are cooking dinner isn't really a good thing. Your attention will be so scattered that none of your activities will be "charged with the grandeur of God," as the Jesuit poet Gerard Manley Hopkins puts it. Instead, everything is reduced to a task to be completed, not part of a life that is being lived.

In order to pray always, we need to focus on one thing at a time. When you are texting on your cell phone, text on your cell phone. When you are making dinner, make dinner. When you are washing the dishes, wash the dishes. The goal is to do one thing at a time, but to do that one thing fully, with all your thoughts and energy focused on it.

Begin by putting your attention on that which is immediately before you. In doing so, you transform the activity from the mundane into something worthy of an offering to the Creator, because God can be met only in the now, only in this breath, only in this intersection of time and space.

Make no mistake: it's not easy to be present in the present moment. Zen masters say we have "monkey minds," which constantly want to swing from one thing to the next, like monkeys looking for ripe bananas. Getting our restless minds to quiet down is an exercise in self-discipline that requires us to surrender our own desires and let go of our racing thoughts.

While it's hard, it's not impossible, as long as we begin in a small way. The next time you wash the dishes, try this experiment. Instead of listening to music or thinking about what comes next, focus all your attention on the process. Look closely at the shape of the glass as you rinse it and place it in the dishwasher. Feel the texture of the pot as you scrub it. Let the warm water run over your fingers. Experience the slipperiness of the soap, the smoothness of the sink, the roughness of the scrubber. As you do, give thanks that you are able to wash the dishes, that you have dishes to wash, that you have eaten a meal that requires dishes to be washed. When you are finished, feel the dryness of the towel as you wipe your hands. Take a towel and wipe the sink dry. Then look into the reflection in the sink and once again, give thanks.

Doing the dishes with this sort of focus might add a minute or two to the entire process, but it will transform what is just another task into a prayer. If you don't believe me, try it for yourself.

Living Prayer

Finally, the last step in praying always is to just do it, as an old Nike ad used to say. We can think about prayer in the abstract, but that's not the same thing as actually praying. We have to harness our thoughts. We have to focus our attention. We have to actually express our gratitude with words, not just a fleeting thought that we should be grateful. Most important, we have to live our lives so that every action is congruent with our belief and trust in a God who loves us. We have to consciously, willingly, desire to pray always and then, when we find ourselves becoming drawn into the things of the world, gently return our intentions to God and eternity.

That's really what praying always means: we turn all of our lives into a hymn of praise, not by what we say, but what we do and how we think. We live in the present so that we can live in eternity.

Once again, as is so often the case, we can't do this of our own accord. We need God's gift of grace to be able to exercise the self-discipline needed to control our thoughts and focus our attention. That's why we ask for the grace to pray always.

I'm always struck by how many paradoxes exist on the spiritual path. The realization that we cannot pray always until we always pray is just one more. By asking God for the grace to be able to pray always—something that he will always give us when we ask—we are finally always able to pray. That's why this is the last grace we ask for . . . and the ultimate gift that God gives us. What more could we aspire to than to live so completely in union with God that our will becomes his will, our desires become his desires, and our lives become his lives? If and when we reach that state, we will no longer need to ask for the grace to pray always, because our every breath will intersect eternity, and we ourselves will become our prayer. In that moment, we will know what heaven truly is.

CHAPTER TEN

O Eternal Father

O Eternal Father, in the name of Jesus.

God.

Eternal Father.

I thought I had moved beyond the limits of age and gender that had me envisioning God as an old Caucasian male with a snowy beard. I thought I had wrapped my mind around the reality that God is neither male nor female, but Eternal Love.

I was wrong. I read a novel in which God was called "Papa," but appeared as a black woman who cooked collard greens and walked barefoot in the garden. The first time "Papa" appeared I was stunned. To say that that image of God upset me is an understatement. With dismay, I realized that I still had God locked in a box that looked like a Renaissance painting by Michelangelo, I think. (Or maybe Raphael.)

Deep down, I really did see God in the most stereotypical fashion, with all the prejudices and limitations that image brings. After struggling for several weeks with my own boxed-in ideas about God, I finally had to ask God to forgive me for turning him into something he wasn't. In fact, I had to ask God to forgive me for always using the masculine pronouns when I thought or wrote about God, although, granted, English doesn't really allow for anything else. (It's just as inaccurate to think of God as "she" or "it" as it is to think of God as exclusively "he." God is God, not a gender-specific pronoun.) I had to ask God to help me see beyond my own limits.

That's where the five graces have come in. They have played an important role in my own journey to understanding and deepening my relationship with God. The graces are more than just a prayer, more than just gifts God wants to give us. They are a way to come to know God as God. Each of the gifts we ask for illuminates an aspect of God that we need to know and provides us with a way we can come into closer, deeper union with God. By asking for these gifts, we are also asking God to be with us in a way that we may never have experienced before.

We Ask Pardon

The first gift is for pardon. We ask God for pardon, not just for our sins, but for having assigned attributes to God that don't belong to him. How many times have we blamed God for the bad things that have happened to us? How frequently have we accused him of being the author of the sorrow into our lives? How often have we thought that God wants us to be in pain, to suffer, to have lack? Instead of believing that God is all loving and all good, we flail at him as if he is taking delight in our misery.

Once we realize what we have done in thinking about—and judging—God in that way, we must also ask him to forgive us for accusing him of being anything less than all good. We must ask his pardon for believing that he has anything other than our best in mind. We must admit that we are guilty of standing in judgment before the Almighty by thinking that he has somehow done us wrong. We must ask forgiveness for assigning blame to the Blameless One and accept our own guilt for doing so in return.

Once we realize that we, created beings that we are, have had the audacity to pretend to judge our Creator, we have taken the first step toward a new relationship with God. Simply by acknowledging that "You are God, and I am not," we open ourselves to the real gifts that God has waited for eternity to bestow on us. But it all begins by asking pardon.

We Ask for Divine Light

Then we ask for the gift of divine light so that we can see God as God. With our limited human abilities, we often cannot see beyond our pain and anger. We are blinded by our sorrow and rage, and we cling to our darkness as if it were a lamp. However, once our lives are illuminated with divine light, we are able to view God's infinite greatness and goodness. When we see with grace, we begin to understand that nothing in this life endures but love, and God is that love, permeating and indwelling in all creation.

The gift of divine light allows us to put aside what older translations of the Bible called the "glass darkly." As 1 Corinthians 13:12 puts it, "At present we see indistinctly, as in a mirror, but then face to face. At present I know partially; then I shall know fully, as I am fully known." Divine light is the gift that allows us the true sight that enables us to see beyond the lures of this life into the enduring lessons and treasures of the next. It is the gift that helps us, like St. Paul, to let the scales fall from our eyes so that we can see clearly. Without divine light, we can never truly be with God. With it, we can never truly be without him.

We Ask a Share of God's Love

Next we ask for a share of God's love, so that our will becomes the same as God's will. Unless we feel loved by God, we will always expect that what he wants and what we want are not going to be the same thing. We will always assume that God is going to make us do things we don't want to do. A Protestant minister friend of mine told me that her greatest fear was that God was going to want her to become a missionary in New Guinea. She was always a little bit afraid to love God because she figured as soon as she told him she loved him, she'd be dropped on the next boat deep within the rain forest. Once she understood that God's love doesn't mean becoming miserable, she also realized that she would be a dreadful foreign missionary and that God would never call her to that life.

However, conforming our will and desires to God's will and desires for us is the only path to happiness. When we live outside of God's will, we may experience the fleeting happiness that the world offers, but we will never be fully content. We will always experience, on the deepest level, a sense that we are lacking something. Once we feel a share of God's love, we know beyond knowing that what he wants for us is so much better than anything we can want for ourselves.

Then we are willing—and able—to surrender our desires to his will. If it had been God's will that my friend be a foreign missionary, she would have experienced peace at the idea, not horror. Safe to say that if you are feeling dread or horror about something you think God is asking of you, it's probably not God's will for your life. Remember, Jesus said, "My peace I give to you" (John 14:27). A sensation of peace is one of the ways we know when we are in God's will. Conversely, a feeling of disquiet or disturbance is a strong clue to stop, reevaluate, and reconsider before taking any action.

Sharing in God's love and being in his will is the secret to why the saints could be joyful even in miserable surroundings. They were so fully in accord with God's will that their lives became a reflection of God's design. It didn't matter if they were sick or well, wealthy or poor. Because they knew they were living the life God wanted for them, they were content. As St. Paul explains,

> I have learned, in whatever situation I find myself, to be self-sufficient. I know indeed how to live in humble circum-stances; I know also how to live with abundance. In every circumstance and in all things I have learned the secret of being well fed and of going hungry, of living in abundance and of being in need. I have the strength for everything through him who empowers me. (Philippians 4:11-13)

Without God and his love, we have no strength. With it, we have all the strength we need, not just to endure in this life, but to triumph in it. God's love is always there for us, but we must ask. He will give, but our part is to request it. As James 4:2 puts it, "You want something and do not have it. . . .You do not have, because you do not ask" (NRSV). So let us ask always.

We Ask for Confidence

In the fourth grace, we ask for the confidence to know that we are not alone in this life. It is the greatest fear of all humanity to be completely and utterly alone. However, as this grace says, through the actions of Jesus, we truly are brothers and sisters. We need to be able to believe, with heart and mind, that we are all children of one God.

Moreover, just as Jesus and his mother Mary intercede for us, we can intercede for others. Through prayer, we are united with all who live here now and all who have gone before us. The artificial boundaries of time and space fall away, and we become centered in the eternal now, which is, after all, the only place where God exists. We ask to be able to place ourselves into that now, so that all we are and all we desire is united in the divine will.

This grace reassures us that we are never truly alone as long as we remember to turn to God in our every hour of every need. With it, we can be assured, confident, that at no point in our lives will we ever be abandoned by our God.

We Ask for Perseverance

Finally, as we approach our God, we ask for perseverance, the grace to live our lives so that we become the people God sees when he looks at us. We see our failures, but God sees us as beloved sons and daughters. Because of our human natures, we will fall and we will fail, but the grace of perseverance allows us to ask to start over. We ask forgiveness for what we have done and failed to do. In his mercy, God erases all our failures and gives us a fresh start. Each day is a new beginning. Each day is a new grace. Yet, we need to ask, and ask again. We need to persevere in our asking so that we can continually start over, confident that God will be there to sustain us, even when we fail again.

One of my favorite sayings is, "Keep on keeping on." I know each morning when I awaken that I will probably fail to live up to my potential that day, but with the gift of perseverance, I start over—and over and over—as many times as it takes. I know that as long as I "keep on keeping on," my God will be there, giving me the strength I need. And I know that even when my own strength flags, his power will be there for me . . . as long as I ask for perseverance.

Back to the Beginning

Eternal Father, your Son has promised that you would grant all the graces we ask of you in his name. Trusting in this promise, and in the name of and through the merits of Jesus Christ, I ask of you five special graces:

First, I ask pardon for all the offenses I have committed, for which I am sorry with all my heart, because I have offended your infinite goodness.

Second, I ask for your divine light, which will enable me to see the vanity of all the things of this earth, and see also your infinite greatness and goodness.

Third, I ask for a share in your love, so that I can detach myself from all creatures, especially from myself, and love only your holy will.

Fourth, grant me the grace to have confidence in the merits of Jesus Christ and in the intercession of Mary.

Fifth, I ask for the grace of perseverance, knowing that whenever I call on you for assistance, you will answer my call and come to my aid;

I fear only that I will neglect to turn to you in time of need, and thus bring myself to ruin.

Grant me the grace to pray always, O Eternal Father, in the name of Jesus.

As I said at the beginning of this book, the prayer of the Five Graces has changed my life and the way I relate to God, but not in the way I expected. My life didn't become all sweetness and light once I prayed for these gifts. On the contrary, I have experienced more trials and difficulties than I could ever imagine, ranging from chronic illness to problems with finances and relationships.

On the surface, it would appear that asking for these graces opened the floodgates to suffering instead of blessings, and believe me, I've been tempted to think that a time or two. But when I settle my fears and worries, I realize that this is just an illusion. We have been told that as long as we live in this world, we will suffer. As long as we have the choice between good and evil, evil will exist, and the existence of evil means that we will all experience pain and suffering. What has happened is not a result of praying the Five Graces, but the result of living in this world. It's just that simple.

Fortunately, God didn't let me give up. I continued to pray the Five Graces, and as I continued, I was positively changed, even as circumstances sometimes grew more negative. As a result of the prayer, I began to understand, on a level that I never had before, that nothing in this life is permanent, save the love of God. In a way that I had never experienced before, I came to know on a soul-deep level that God doesn't bring us trials, but that God is always with us during the trials. Gradually, I began to be able to accept the negative things that entered my life, not as a punishment extended by a mean and crabby God, but as a way of correcting my direction. I knew I had reached a new level, when my first thought as something unpleasant happened was not, "O God, why me?" but "O, God, what lesson do you want me to learn in this?"

Once I was able to accept the circumstances of my life as a way for God to teach me more about him and his creation, I was better able to see that all things really do work together for good for those who love the Lord. The Five Graces allowed me to relax in the knowledge that not only wasn't I in charge, but that I didn't need to be. God knows what is coming and has already prepared the way for me. When I wander off the path, God uses whatever means are necessary to bring me back, but always because he loves me and wants my ultimate happiness.

Obviously I don't know where my journey will go from here. None of us do. I only know that as I accept the gifts of pardon, divine light, God's love, confidence, and perseverance, I am at peace with whatever comes next. I am content to wait and watch to see how the Lord will work in my life, what doors he will open, what events he will allow, and what new opportunities to love he will bring to me.

I hope and pray the same for each of you.